THE LITTLE BOOK OF
LYKKE

THE LITTLE BOOK OF

LYKKE

THE DANISH SEARCH FOR THE WORLD'S HAPPIEST PEOPLE

MEIK WIKING

PENGUIN LIFE

AN IMPRINT OF

PENGUIN BOOKS

PENGUIN LIFE

UK | USA | Canada | Ireland | Australia
India | New Zealand | South Africa

Penguin Life is part of the Penguin Random House
group of companies whose addresses can be found at
global.penguinrandomhouse.com

First pu

001

Copyri

The mo

Quote from *The Two Towers* by J.R.R. Tolkien © the Tolkien Estate
Limited, 1954, 1955, 1966. Reprinted by permission of HarperCollins
Publishers Ltd.

Designed by Hampton Associates
Colour reproduction by Born
Printed in Italy by Printer Trento S.r.l.

A CIP catalogue record for this book is available from the British Library

ISBN: 978-0-241-30201-9

MIX
Paper from
responsible sources
FSC
www.fsc.org
FSC® C018179

Penguin Random House is committed to a
sustainable future for our business, our readers
and our planet. This book is made from Forest
Stewardship Council® certified paper.

CONTENTS

CHAPTER ONE

THE TREASURE HUNT

THE TREASURE HUNT

'What are we holding on to, Sam?'

*'That there's some good in this world, Mr Frodo.
And it's worth fighting for.'*

Like Tolkien, Hemingway once wrote that the world is a fine place
and worth fighting for. These days, it is easier to notice the fighting
rather than what is fine. It is easy to point towards the grey skies and
dark clouds, but perhaps we all need to be more like Samwise the
Stout-hearted (but preferably a bit less furry in the feet department)
and see what is good in this world of ours.

A friend of mine, Rita, grew up in Latvia during the Soviet era. It
may not have been Mordor, but it was a time of fear and mistrust,
a time when every window was covered with a curtain and when
communities were shaped by suspicion and scarcity. Occasionally,
a truck carrying bananas would arrive from Vietnam. Not knowing
when bananas would be available again, my friend and her family
would buy as many as they could afford and could carry.

Then the waiting would begin, as the bananas would still be green
and not ready to eat. They would place the fruit in a dark cabinet to
make it ripen faster. Watching bananas turn from green to yellow
was like magic in a city that was fifty shades of grey. As a child,

Rita had thought only three colours existed: black, grey and brown. Her dad decided to change that and he took her on a treasure hunt around the city: to look for colour, for beauty and for the good in the world.

This is the intention of this book: to take you treasure hunting; to go in pursuit of happiness; to find the good that does exist in this world – and to bring this into the light so that, together, we can help it spread. Books are wonderful idea-spreaders. My previous book, *The Little Book of Hygge*, shared the Danish concept of everyday happiness with the world. The book encouraged its readers to focus on the simple pleasures in life and, since its publication, I have received an avalanche of kind letters from around the world.

LYKKE

LUUH

KAH

One of them was from Sarah, who teaches five-year-olds in the UK and has long had an interest in the mental health of children and how happiness has an impact on their capacity to learn. 'I have read your book and decided to introduce *hygge* into my classroom,' she wrote. She told me how the class put up fairy lights, shared snacks, lit a candle and enjoyed story-time. 'We even put a YouTube video of a log fire on our interactive whiteboard to make it feel cosier. On these long winter days which seem so dreary after Christmas, it is cheering up the whole class and staff no end. I am trying to figure out how to measure the impact of this on the children's well-being, but I guess the relaxed, smiling faces are measure enough!'

That is essentially my job as CEO of the Happiness Research Institute in Copenhagen: to measure, understand and generate happiness. At the institute, we explore the causes and effects of human happiness and work towards improving the quality of life of people across the world.

My work has allowed me to talk to people from all four corners of the earth: from Copenhagen mayors to Mexican street food vendors, from Indian cab drivers to the Minister of Happiness in the United Arab Emirates. It has taught me two things. First of all, that we may be Danish, Mexican, Indian, Emirati, or any other nationality, but we are first and foremost humans. We are not as different from each other as we may think. The hopes of those in Copenhagen and Guadalajara and the dreams of those in New York, Delhi and Dubai all point towards the same beacon: happiness. *Lykke* is the Danish word for 'happiness', but you might refer to it as *felicidad* if you are Spanish, or *Glück* or *bonheur* if you are German or French. No matter what you call it, story-time will light up smiles in classrooms in the same way wherever you are in the world.

A couple of years ago, I was skiing with some friends in Italy. We had finished for the day and were enjoying the sun and coffee on the balcony of our cabin. Then somebody realized that we had leftover pizza in the fridge, and I exclaimed: 'Is this happiness? I think so.' And I wasn't the only one. Despite the fact that my friends on the balcony were from different countries – Denmark, India and the US – we all felt that sharing food with friends in the soft warmth of a March sun, overlooking the beautiful, snow-covered mountains, was pretty damn close to happiness. We might have been born on different continents, raised in different cultures, schooled in different languages, but we all shared the same feeling that this was happiness.

On a much bigger and more scientific scale, this is what we can use happiness data to understand. What do happy people have in common? Whether you are from Denmark, the US or India, what are the common denominators of happiness? We have been doing this kind of research for years in terms of health: for example, what are the common denominators for those people who live to be a hundred years old? Because of these studies, we know that alcohol, tobacco, exercise and our diet all have an effect on life expectancy. At the Happiness Research Institute, we use the same methods to understand what it is that matters for happiness, life satisfaction and quality of life.

Allow me to take you to the home of the Happiness Research Institute – the capital of happiness: Copenhagen.

DENMARK: THE
HAPPINESS SUPERPOWER?

––––––––

It is four o'clock in the afternoon in Copenhagen. The streets are alive with cyclists, as people leave the office to pick up their children from school.

A couple who are sharing their fifty-two weeks of paid maternity and paternity leave are strolling along the waterfront. A group of students are swimming in the clean water in the harbour, carefree, because not only are there no university tuition fees, students also receive the equivalent of £590 (after tax) every month from the government. Everything runs smoothly in Denmark. Well, almost. Four years ago, one train did arrive five minutes late. The passengers each got a letter of apology from the prime minister and a designer chair of their choice as compensation.

With headlines like these over the last ten years, it may be easy to imagine Denmark as some sort of utopia.

*Denmark – The World's
Happiest Country*

*Copenhagen:
The Happy Capital*

*Denmark, Where Joy
is Always in Season*

*The Happiest Place
in the World*

*Denmark: Officially the
Happiest Country in
the World. Again.*

*World Happiness Report:
You Should Live in
Denmark*

Let's get one thing out of the way: I am a big fan of Denmark, both as a happiness scientist and as a citizen. When I see seven-year-old children cycle safely to school on their own, I smile. When I see parents leaving their kids to sleep unsupervised outside cafés in strollers without worrying about it, I smile. When I see people swimming in the clean water of the inner harbour of Copenhagen, I smile.

To me, it is unsurprising that a peaceful country, where there is free and universal health care, where your kids can go to university no matter how much money you earn and where little girls can imagine themselves prime minister should be one of the happiest countries in the world, according to the World Happiness Reports commissioned by the United Nations.

But does this mean that Denmark is a perfect society? No. Do I think that Denmark provides *relatively* good conditions for its citizens to enjoy a *relatively* high level of quality of life and happiness? Yes. I also believe that Japan had the longest average life expectancy in the world last year, but it doesn't mean that I think that every Japanese person lives to exactly 83.7 years of age.

Denmark may usually top the lists of the world's happiest countries, but it is important to understand that these rankings are based on averages. For instance, in the latest World Happiness Report, Danes reported an average of 7.5 on a scale from 0 to 10.

It also means that while some things work extremely well, other things are rotten in the state of Denmark. Scandinavian countries may do well in the happiness rankings – but neither Danes, Norwegians nor Swedes hold a monopoly on happiness. Living in Denmark has taught me that, while we can all learn a lot from the

Scandinavian countries when it comes to quality of life, we can find lessons in happiness from people from all over the world. The keys to happiness are buried around the world, and it is our job to gather them up.

If we look at the World Happiness Report, there is a four-point happiness gap between the happiest and unhappiest countries, and three points of these four are explained by six factors: togetherness or sense of community, money, health, freedom, trust and kindness. I have dedicated one chapter to each of these factors, and in each we will explore why these things affect well-being, we will take lessons of happiness from people from around the world and we will uncover the ways in which we ourselves may become happier – and, in the end, how we may put these pieces together to create a treasure map of happiness.

Meanwhile, 80 per cent of the difference in happiness across the world happens *within* countries. In other words, you may find very happy Danes and very unhappy Danes – and you may find very happy and very unhappy Togolese. So it is one thing to look at the policies countries offer; our behaviour and our perspective on life are another thing entirely.

So, what are the common denominators among the world's happiest people, what can be learned from countries around the globe when it comes to happiness and what actions may be taken in order to make ourselves happier? These are some of the questions this book seeks to answer: it will uncover the secrets of the world's happiest people and look for the good that does exist in the world. Let's go on a treasure hunt!

—

CHAPTER TWO

HOW DO YOU MEASURE HAPPINESS?

H O W   D O   Y O U
M E A S U R E   H A P P I N E S S ?

On the morning of 9 November 2016, I was woken at 5 a.m. by the emergency alarm in the hotel I was staying in. I was in the heart of Paris for a round of interviews and the city was approaching the first anniversary of the terrorist attacks on the city.

Outside the lobby, the guests gathered, bleary-eyed, in their white bathrobes. At 5.30 a.m., the hotel was given the all-clear, but there was no point in me trying to get back to sleep. Adrenalin was still pumping through me, and I had just returned from Asia, so my body clock was seven hours ahead of local time. I decided I might as well work and opened my suitcase to get my laptop. That's when I discovered I had left my brand-new computer on the plane (always check the seat pocket!). And I hadn't backed up the first chapters of this book anywhere other than on the now missing laptop.

I was frustrated, tired and angry with myself. I thought I could do with some good news and realized the votes would by now have been counted in the US presidential election and I thought it might cheer me up to see the victory speech of the first female US president, so I turned on the news.

That day I had eight interviews lined up. Eight journalists, who would most likely all ask the question: 'You study happiness – so how happy are you?'

So, how happy was I? Can you quantify feelings? How do we measure happiness?

The way the world has been measuring happiness for decades can be summed up like this: Imagine two friends meeting after a long time. 'How are you?' the one friend asks the other. 'I make 40,800 euros per year,' she replies. No one talks like this, but this is how we have been measuring well-being traditionally. We have been saying that money equals happiness. And while money may matter – it is not the only thing that contributes to our happiness.

Unfortunately, that is how we have been measuring happiness up until recently. We have been using income as a proxy for happiness, well-being or quality of life and using GDP per capita to measure our progress as nations. One of the reasons for this is that income – national or personal – is objective. However, happiness is not. Happiness is subjective.

This is often the first response I get when people hear that the Happiness Research Institute tries to measure happiness:

'How can you measure happiness, it is so subjective?'

Yes, of course happiness is subjective, and it should be. To me, that is not an issue. What I care about in my research is how *you* feel about *your* life. That is what counts. I believe you are the best judge of whether you are happy or not. How you feel is our new metric – and then I try to understand why you feel that way. If you are happier than your neighbour, who has the bigger house, the fancy car and the perfect spouse, by our measures, you are the one that is doing something right.

Working with subjective measures is difficult, but it is not impossible. We do it all the time when it comes to stress, anxiety and depression, which are also subjective phenomena. At the end of the day, it is all about how we as individuals perceive our lives.

Happiness can mean different things to different people. You may have one perception of what happiness is, I may have another. Right now, we put the happiness label on different things, which, from a scientific point of view, makes it difficult to work around. So, the first thing we must do is to break the concept of happiness down into its various parts.

For instance, if we were to look at how the economy is doing, we could break it down into indicators such as GDP, growth and interest and unemployment rates. Each indicator gives us additional information about how the economy is doing. The same thing goes for happiness. It is an umbrella term. So, we break it down and look at the different components. Let's go back to that morning in Paris. How happy was I?

When we look at how I was feeling at that moment, I was angry with myself for forgetting the computer, I was tired, and I was sad to hear that a lot of Americans would be facing four difficult years. In short, I was angry, tired and sad. Happy? Not so much, and pretty far from sitting on a sun-bathed balcony in the Alps eating leftover pizza with friends. On the other hand, I was in the middle of a book tour and had the privilege of talking to people around the world about my work and about happiness, so, overall, life was not treating me badly.

THE THREE DIMENSIONS
OF HAPPINESS

The first lesson in happiness research is to distinguish between being happy right now and being happy overall. We call these two states, respectively, the **affective dimension** *and the* **cognitive dimension**.

The affective – or hedonic – dimension examines the emotions people experience on an everyday basis. If you look at yesterday, were you depressed, sad, anxious, worried? Did you laugh? Did you feel happy? Did you feel loved?

In order to look at the cognitive dimension, people have to take a step back and evaluate their lives. How satisfied are you with your life *overall*? How happy are you in general? Think of the best possible life you could lead, and the worst possible. Where do you feel you stand right now? For you, the best possible life imaginable may involve fame and fortune, or it might mean staying at home to home-school your kids. To me, those are equally valid dreams. When trying to evaluate happiness, the important information is what your dream is and how close you feel to living that dream.

Of course, the affective and cognitive dimensions are connected, and they do overlap to some extent. If your days are filled with positive emotions, you are likely to report higher levels of overall life satisfaction. Equally, we can have shitty mornings and still feel we have a wonderful life overall.

To make things a little more complicated, let me introduce a third dimension called **eudaimonia**. That is the Ancient Greek word for happiness, and it is based on Aristotle's perception of happiness. To him, the good life was a meaningful and purposeful life. In this book, I will mainly focus on overall happiness – the cognitive dimension – people who feel they have a wonderful life, but we will look at our everyday moods and our sense of purpose as well.

Once we have looked at these three dimensions, what we at the Happiness Research Institute ideally do is to follow people over time. Not in a creepy, stalker kind of way but scientifically.

We monitor large groups of people over long periods of time to see how changes in their lives impact on their happiness. If I were to follow you and ten thousand other people, some significant changes are bound to happen to each individual over the next decade that will make a difference to how happy they are. Some of them will fall in love and some will fall out of love; some will be promoted and some will be fired; some will move to London and some will leave the city; some will break hearts and some will have their hearts broken. Over the next ten years, highs and lows are guaranteed, we are bound to witness victories and losses – and at least one distrait, elbow-patch-wearing scientist will leave his computer on a plane. The question is, how do those events and changes in life circumstance impact on the different dimensions of happiness? What is the average impact on people's life satisfaction from doubling their income, getting married or moving to the countryside? *That* is what we try to understand.

The combined average of World Happiness Reports
2013-2017

1st	2nd	3rd
Denmark	Switzerland	Norway
7.57	**7.56**	**7.55**

Average happiness rating on a scale of 0 to 10

Iceland: **7.48**

Finland: **7.41**

Canada: **7.4**

Netherlands: **7.4**

Sweden: **7.35**

Australia: **7.3**

New Zealand: **7.28**

Israel: **7.26**

Austria: **7.17**

Costa Rica: **7.16**

United States: **7.07**

Puerto Rico: **7.03**

Ireland: **6.97**

Luxembourg: **6.93**

Belgium: **6.93**

Mexico: **6.9**

Brazil: **6.85**

Oman: **6.85**

Germany: **6.84**

United Arab Emirates: **6.81**

UK: **6.79**

Panama: **6.77**

Singapore: **6.66**

Chile: **6.65**

It is not easy. While you may observe that, in general, people living in the countryside are happier than people living in big cities – and perhaps it is true that people's happiness increases if they move to the countryside – we can't always be certain about what is the cause and what is the effect. Perhaps people who move to and live in the big cities are less happy not because of the big city but because of the type of person you are if you choose to live in a big city. Perhaps people who are attracted to big cities are more ambitious, and the downside to being ambitious is that you are chronically dissatisfied with the status quo. Ideally, we would undertake experiments with identical twins, separate them at birth and flip a coin to see which twin should grow up and live for the rest of their life in the city and which in the countryside. But the government says that I'm not allowed to do that.

In other words, there are a lot of things we cannot control for and there are a lot of pitfalls in the science of happiness. But the best way to make sure that we do *not* gain knowledge in this field is to lean back and say that it can't be done. I am yet to hear a convincing argument why happiness should be the one thing in the world we cannot study in a scientific manner. And yes, it may be easier to sit in our armchairs with our arms crossed, insisting that it can't be done – but those sorts of people have never discovered new continents or taken man to the moon. What makes me proud to be part of the human race – with all our faults and failures – is our endless curiosity and imagination. We are the only species who will look towards a red, barren planet in the distant sky and think, how do we get up there? So why should we not try to push the boundaries for quality of life? What I see is a big potential to improve happiness through little adjustments in our behaviour. Great things sometimes have small beginnings.

CHAPTER THREE

TOGETHERNESS

RITUALS OF
FOOD AND FIRE

Across from the cabin where I spent my childhood summers, there was an open field of grass. The grass would grow so tall that my brother and I could create tunnels in this green blanket and play there for hours. Some time in June, the field would be mown, and that smell of freshly cut grass will forever transport me back to those days.

The grass would be collected into bales of hay, which would slowly turn yellow under the midsummer sun. Back then, I was sure these were in fact big pieces of Lego forgotten by *jætter* – the supernatural giants of Norse mythology. Nevertheless, that did not stop me and the other kids on the street from building houses and labyrinths out of them before the field was cleared to make room for the summer solstice bonfire. The summer solstice may be a pagan ritual, but to this day it remains my favourite tradition. The Nordic sun sets into a night without darkness and the bonfires are lit throughout the country to celebrate midsummer. Remember: Danes are the direct descendants of Vikings, so we enjoy watching things burn: bonfires, candles, villages. It's all good.

I am not sure I *knew* what happiness was then, standing there with my bare feet in the grass, my face warmed by the fire, a piece of freshly baked bread in my hand and my parents' hands on my shoulders, but I am sure I *felt* what I would later dedicate my career to understanding. As a child, I did not have the words to describe it, but I am sure that, as well as happiness, I felt a sense of community, a sense of belonging, a sense of home. This was my tribe.

The capacity of fire and food to bring people together is almost universal across cultures and geographical borders. And sometimes, we need do no more than light a candle to create a sense of community around our dinner tables.

'I almost forgot to tell you,' Janic said. He is a Canadian journalist who had just interviewed me at the Happiness Research Institute in Copenhagen. 'After I read about *hygge*, I went out and bought these two chandeliers and we started lighting them at dinner.' Janic and his wife have three sons: eighteen-year-old twins and a son who is fifteen. 'At first, when I started lighting the candles for dinner, the boys were like, "Hey, what's going on? What's with the romance? Do you want to have dinner alone with Mum?" There was an adjustment period, then *they* started to light the candles for dinner. But, more importantly, I have noticed that our family dinners are now fifteen to twenty minutes longer, because – how can I describe this? – the candles put the boys in a story-telling mood. They don't just shovel in the food any more, they sip their wine, they tell us about their day.' Dinnertime is no longer just about food – it is about togetherness.

Our languages are reminders that sharing food nurtures more than our physical body. It feeds our friendships, bolsters our bonds and nourishes our sense of community – and those factors are vital to our happiness.

Whether you look at the English word 'companion', the Spanish word compañero *or the French* copain, *they all originate from the Latin* com *and* panis, *meaning 'with whom one shares bread'.*

Starting out with the rituals of food and fire around the dinner table can ignite an understanding that the good life builds on connection and purpose. That our wealth is not measured by the size of our bank accounts but by the strength of our bonds, the health of our loved ones and the level of our gratitude. That happiness does not come from owning a bigger car but from knowing that we are part of something bigger – part of a community – and that we are all in this together.

What we at both the Happiness Research Institute and the World Happiness Report find is that the happiest countries have a strong sense of community, and the happiest people have someone they can rely on in times of need. That is why it is no coincidence that Danes are not only among the happiest in the world but are also among the ones who meet most often with their friends and family and trust that their friends will catch them if they fall.

Percentage of people who believe they can rely on their friends in times of need

New Zealand: **98.6%**

Iceland: **95.7%**

Denmark: **95.5%**

Spain: **95.5%**

Ireland: **95.3%**

Australia: **95.1%**

Finland: **94.2%**

Canada: **93.9%**

Switzerland: **93.5%**

United Kingdom: **93.4%**

Luxembourg: **93.4%**

Norway: **93.1%**

Austria: **92.5%**

Sweden: **92.3%**

Germany: **92.3%**

Slovak Republic: **92.2%**

Japan: **91.0%**

Russian Federation: **90.7%**

Italy: **90.7%**

Czech Republic: **90.3%**

Estonia: **90.2%**

United States: **90.1%**

Brazil: **90.0%**

South Africa: **89.5%**

France: **89.4%**

Slovenia: **88.9%**

Belgium: **88.4%**

Netherlands: **87.9%**

Poland: **86.3%**

Israel: **85.7%**

Portugal: **85.1%**

Latvia: **84.2%**

Turkey: **83.6%**

Greece: **83.4%**

Chile: **82.5%**

Hungary: **82.2%**

Korea: **75.8%**

Mexico: **75.3%**

Source: OECD, Better Life Index 2016

EAT LIKE THE FRENCH – CREATE RITUALS OF FOOD AND FIRE

Make time to eat. Reclaim your lunchtime and sit with friends, family and colleagues, and enjoy eating your food slowly and with company.

'And for dessert?'

'No dessert, but I would like a coffee afterwards, please. *Un café américain.*'

After giving a lecture in Paris, I had the afternoon off and had lunch in a small restaurant close to the Musée d'Orsay, on the border between the 5th and 7th arrondissements.

'No dessert, and you order American coffee in Paris. You are a brave man,' the waiter replied with a smile.

Food is not taken lightly in France. This is perhaps most evident in their state schools. Kids are served three-course meals that may consist of a salad for starters, a main course of veal marinated with mushrooms and broccoli, and apple tart for dessert – and cheese and bread, of course. The cloth napkins and the genuine silverware reveal that the ritual around the meal is almost as important as the food itself. It is about sitting down and eating calmly. The French eat together. That might be one of the reasons why the French are the ones who spend most time eating each day. And, despite its population having three courses and spending all that time at the table, France still has some of the lowest obesity levels in Europe. This may be due to the fact that people eat more when they sit in front of the TV.

According to a study from the University of Liverpool, published in the *American Journal of Clinical Nutrition*, it could be as much as 25 per cent more. And while most countries have official diet recommendations about how many portions of fruit and vegetables we should eat per day, one of the official recommendations in France is that you should eat with other people. That is one thing we could all aspire to do more frequently.

THE GOOD LIFE AND THE COMMON GOOD

In the past five years, I have spoken to more than a thousand people about why Denmark, and Scandinavia more generally, do well in the happiness rankings. Often, people will say, 'Danes pay some of the highest taxes in the world, so why are they so happy?'

And yes, Denmark has one of the highest tax rates in the world. The average income in Denmark is about 39,000 euros per year and the average Dane pays around 45 per cent in income taxes. If you make more than 61,500 euros per year, there is an additional tax rate – making it 52 per cent over this threshold.

However, I believe the Danes are happy not *despite* the high taxes but *because* of the high taxes – and most Danes would agree. Almost nine out of ten people living in Denmark say they happily pay their taxes, according to a Gallup survey undertaken in 2014. It's all about knowing that happiness does not come from owning a bigger car but from knowing that everybody you know and love will be supported in their time of need. What works well in the Nordic countries is an understanding of the link between the good life and the common good. We are not paying taxes; we are purchasing quality of life. We are investing in our community.

9 out of 10 people living in Denmark say they happily pay their taxes

In Danish, the word for community is *fællesskab*. *Fællesskab* can be split up into *fælles*, meaning 'common' or 'shared', and *skab*, which can mean either 'cabinet' or 'create'. Not only is community our common cabinet (our shared supplies), it is also something we create together. I think there is some beauty in that.

Like the Germans, we Danes love compound words. Maybe it is because of the cold climate, but Danish words like to spoon. *Råstofproduktionsopgørelsesskemaudfyldningsvejledning* is the word for a manual to fill out a questionnaire about the production of raw materials. It is also the reason why Scrabble in Denmark is considered an extreme sport and is the number-one cause of wrist injuries. There are seventy words in the official Danish dictionary by the Society for Danish Language and Literature that have the word *fællesskab* in them.

We talk about . . .

Bofællesskab:
A co-housing scheme

Fællesgrav:
A shared grave, e.g. where several people are buried together

Fællesskabsfølelse:
A sense of community

Fællesøkonomi:
A shared economy, e.g. when couples have a joint bank account

Skæbnefællesskab:
A shared destiny

Fællesskøn:
A shared gender. Whereas most languages divide nouns into masculine and feminine, Danish nouns are divided into no-gender and common-gender – they are the hermaphrodites of nouns, if you will.

BOFÆLLESSKAB - HAPPINESS OF THE COMMONS

The houses form an open circle around the common yard. It is June, there is a crisp blue sky, and the garden is alive with the sounds of children playing. Children from different families are running in and out of the houses.

Unlike most kids these days, these boys and girls are growing up with an unusual combination of freedom and security. Some of them are playing *kubb* – a lawn game said to have originated in the Viking age, in which you throw sticks at other sticks. A dog is watching, as if the game were the greatest invention ever. Other kids are gathered around a campfire with a couple of grown-ups.

'Hi, Mikkel, you bandit!' one of the men calls out, and smiles at us. Jørgen is one of the residents here and knows my friend Mikkel well.

Mikkel grew up here. He lives in Copenhagen now but, last summer, we returned to his childhood home to pick up his dad to go on our annual sailing trip. They sail; I photograph, and insist on calling the pictures 'sailfies'. Despite this, I am invited to join them again every year. We cannot park next to the house because the parking spots are on the fringe of this little community, so you walk the last forty metres on foot, across the common yard, to get to Mikkel's parents' house. That is no coincidence: the area is designed to encourage social interaction and impromptu conversation between residents.

The place is called Fælleshaven. Yes, it is another compound word. *Fælles* means 'common' and *haven* means 'garden'. It is a *bofællesskab*. *Fællesskab* means 'community' and *bo* means 'to live'. A *bofællesskab* is a co-housing scheme which originated in Denmark but rapidly spread to the rest of Scandinavia and onwards.

The initiators were families and individuals who were discontent with then current ways of living. One of them was Bodil Graa, who wrote an opinion piece called 'Children Should Have One Hundred Parents' in one of the major papers in Denmark and asked for like-minded people to get in touch with her. Many did and, five years later, in 1972, the construction of the *bofællesskab* Sætterdammen was finished. It consisted of twenty-seven independent houses and a large common house and is situated near Hillerød, north of Copenhagen. It still exists today, and seventy people live there. They have a waiting list of those who would like to buy vacant homes. Today, around fifty thousand people live in co-housing in Denmark and it is still growing in popularity.

One of the hundreds of Danish *bofællesskaber* is Fælleshaven, where my friend Mikkel grew up. It is home to sixteen families, among them twenty children. The *bofællesskab* is designed for privacy as well as community. It means that each family has a private home with all the traditional amenities, including its own private kitchen. Yet the private homes are clustered around a shared space – a garden and a large communal kitchen and dining area. The families live separately, yet together.

If they feel like it, from Monday to Thursday the families eat together. Usually, there are between thirty and forty people at these dinners; a meal for an adult costs around 20 kroner (approximately £2.25) and those for kids are half price. To give you an idea of how little this is, I can tell you that a café latte in Copenhagen will set you back 40 kroner.

But it is not the price of the communal meals that is appealing to most people here. Especially for the families with young children, it is the fact that, four nights a week, there is no logistical juggling act of grocery shopping and preparing dinner. Instead, they help the kids with their homework, play *kubb* or teach them how to build a good campfire. One week every six months or so, they form part of the crew who prepares the dinner, and the older kids help out and learn how to cook. The food shift usually takes three hours, from preparing the food until the dishes are finished – obviously, with a break to eat dinner and a cup of coffee afterwards. But on most nights, residents at Fælleshaven can relax and wait for the bell that tells them dinner is ready.

Besides the dining area and the campfire, Fælleshaven also has a shared vegetable garden, a playground and playing field, an art studio, a workshop and spare guestrooms if people have too many guests to put up in their own homes. The set-up also means that the children always have someone to play with. Not once have the families had a need to hire a babysitter. If the parents want to go to the cinema or see a play, they just send their kids to their friends across the yard.

According to the Office of National Statistics in Denmark, the number of *bofællesskaber* has increased by 20 per cent in the past six years. It is especially attractive to families looking for supportive environments for their kids, and to elderly relatives, who are in danger of falling into social isolation.

A couple of years ago, the Danish anthropologist Max Pedersen did a large study of *seniorbofælleskaber*, co-housing for the elderly, and found that 'it is difficult to see the data and statements as other than a success for the *bofælleskaber*': 98 per cent reported feeling safe in their community, 95 per cent were satisfied with their living situation – but I think the most interesting data was that 70 per cent reported having at least four friends among their neighbours.

What about you? Do you know the names of your neighbours – and would you call any of them your friends?

How many of your neighbours would you describe as friends?

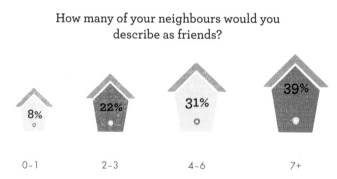

| 0 – 1 | 2 – 3 | 4 – 6 | 7+ |

Number of neighbours described as friends by Danes living in *bofælleskaber*

Source: Max Pedersen, The Great Experiment *(Det store eksperiment), 2013*

The *bofælleskaber* scheme is now gaining momentum around the world, and increasing in popularity in Canada, Australia and Japan. Hundreds have already been established in Germany, the US and the Netherlands. In 2014, the *Guardian* reported that more than sixty co-housing projects were in the pipeline in the United Kingdom. Jo Gooding, coordinator of the UK Co-housing Network, describes these projects as 'self-managing communities, independently governed by the people who live there'.

Like the place where Mikkel grew up, the design encourages social interaction and attracts single elderly people who want to live neither in isolation nor in conventional housing for old people, and families who gain when raising their kids and working at a career by living in a supportive environment. According to the *Guardian*, there was a 100 per cent increase in groups forming between 2012 and 2014, and at least eighteen projects have been completed, with 'a definite trend towards cities', including London, Cardiff, Newcastle, Leeds and Cambridge.

As a happiness researcher, that makes me, well, happy. But you do not need to be a happiness researcher to guess what effect a stronger sense of community, an increased feeling of safety and security and more and closer friendships have on people's happiness.

Naturally, the balance of privacy and communality is critical in these models and a *bofællesskab* is not for everyone, but perhaps we can take elements of what works and apply them in new settings. It's clear that being part of a tribe has a positive effect on our well-being. So, let's look at some concrete steps you can take to enhance the community spirit in your neighbourhood.

FIVE WAYS TO PLANT A COMMUNITY

1. CREATE A DIRECTORY FOR YOUR STREET OR STAIRWAY

Knock on your neighbours' doors and introduce yourself. Alternatively, for us introverts, drop a sign-up sheet in everyone's letterbox. You can tell people that you are creating the list in case of burst pipes and other emergencies. Ask for names and contact information, but also consider adding a questionnaire to help you get to know people better. Would you babysit a dog or cat? (Yes! Also, can I please walk the dog once in a while?) What is your favourite book? (I'm always torn between *The Great Gatsby* and *A Farewell to Arms*.) How many languages do you speak? (Three on average. After a bottle of wine: five; before my morning coffee: barely one.) Try and focus on skills that might be of use to other neighbours. Who is good with computers? Who knows how to change a tyre? Who knows how to preserve fruit?

2. ESTABLISH A BOOK-LENDING CUPBOARD

A simple way to start the conversation in your community is to establish a mini-library built on the take-one-leave-one-book principle. The library doesn't have to be anything fancy or contain the entire collection of the Library of Alexandria.

In my stairway in Copenhagen, I've just put books on top of the rack of letterboxes. It makes the stairway more homely, it is fun to watch which books get picked up and it encourages interaction between the neighbours. The current collection in my stairway includes titles like *A Concise History of Architecture*, *The Great Gatsby* and *Introduction to Statistics*. For some reason, the first two seem to be the most popular.

3. USE THE SOFT EDGES

There is a bench in my courtyard right outside my kitchen window where I often sit and read. From the bench, you can see a tall chestnut tree and hear the wind in the leaves. The bench also functions as a semi-private space – I can be by myself, but I am still close enough to the public space that people will say hello and ask about the book I'm reading. You won't ever get to know your neighbours if you never see them. Spaces like this – front gardens and porches – are called soft edges, and studies show that streets with soft edges feel safer and people tend to stay in them longer. Just being out in front of your house gives a welcoming vibe that encourages interaction. Few people would dare come into your kitchen to say hello, but if you are in your front garden, people may get to know you and you them. Because of my outdoor reading spot, I've learned that, upstairs from me, live Peter and his daughter Katrine, and further up lives Majed, who has a fruit store (with delicious peaches), and the last time I met him he was going on his first bike ride in twenty years. Interestingly, noise from neighbours ceases to be annoying once you get to know their names and stories.

4. BUILD A COMMUNITY GARDEN

Your home may not offer any soft edges, but there might be a strip of land in your neighbourhood that can be used to create a small community garden – a time-tested way not only to grow a bunch of fresh veggies but also to cultivate a sense of community and for you to put down roots. Tending to your tomatoes is not only relaxing and meditative, it brings people in the local neighbourhood together and fosters the development of community spirit. In other words, it is a delicious way of creating a village atmosphere in a big city.

In addition, while more research is still needed, studies suggest that gardening has great benefits for our mental health. There is no magic bullet that cures depression, but sometimes the garden can function as the midpoint between the bed and the outside world, taking us – literally – into the light. A few years ago, the Happiness Research Institute were working for a city in Denmark, developing a strategy to improve quality of life for its citizens, and suggested they established community gardens, as one of the main challenges faced by the city was loneliness in the community. We liked the idea so much we wanted to build one ourselves. So we did. At the time, our office was just across from a church that had spare land, so we bought a truckload of dirt, invited the neighbours, spent one Sunday afternoon building twenty raised plant beds and topped it off with a barbecue.

5. START A TOOL-SHARING PROGRAMME

The average power drill is used for only a few minutes per year, so there is no need for all of us to have one at home. Power drills, hammers, four different kinds of screwdriver – they all take up space; not to mention leaf-blowers and snow-blowers. A tool-sharing programme is also a good excuse to get to know your neighbours. In short, sharing your tools with neighbours leads to more resources, more community spirit and less clutter for everyone. When you are putting together the street directory, you can ask what tools people might be interested in borrowing and lending – or, if there is extra space in the basement, create a 'tool library' board. Put up a board with some tools on it, for example a hammer and screwdriver, and draw around them. Put in a few nails so that the hammer can hang on the board. Also draw the shapes of the tools that are missing so that your neighbours can contribute their excess tools.

CASE STUDY
SHANI

Shani grew up in Gibson, a small town in Canada, where she would sell raspberries in front of her house for pocket money and neighbours would wave to her as she walked to school.

It was the kind of place where nobody locked their doors, but when she was fourteen her family moved to Australia. She became a teacher – and a nomad, moving from country to country, city to city, longing for the connection with other people she remembered from Gibson.

Later on, working as a school administrator in tough schools with tough kids took its toll on Shani, and she became ill. She was burnt out and clinically depressed. While she was broken in spirit, her partner, Tim, was broken in body. Working as a stonemason and sculptor had left its mark on his shoulders, knees and wrists.

They lived on Hulbert Street, a quiet cul-de-sac with thirty-two houses in it. Hulbert Street is in Fremantle, a suburb of Perth in Western Australia, but you could place this street in towns throughout the world and few would notice a difference. It was a normal street, in a normal neighbourhood, in a normal city. Until Shani and Tim ran an environmental education course for their neighbours. Behind it was the idea that community is part of sustainability. Could they turn their street into more of a community?

'What would we like Hulbert Street to be like? If we could do anything – don't worry about money, don't worry about resources, don't worry about who is going to do what – what would we like to see happen in our street?'

The grown-ups dreamt of gardening days and weekly afternoon tea, and the kids dreamt of cricket games and soccer matches in the middle of the street. Then a ten-year-old said, 'I would like a skateboard ramp in the street.' Well, that is never going to happen, Shani thought.

But, in fact, it was the first thing that did happen, thanks to one of the neighbours, who found some materials and had the skills to make the ramp. The skateboard ramp changed the street from a place you drove your car down to a street you played in.

At the same time, the street was plagued by burglaries, and there was some concern – especially for Anna, who was eighty-four and living by herself at the end of the street. 'So we developed what we call the Hulbert Street skill register. It was a contact list initially, but it stretched beyond that: what do you have to share – and what do you need,' Shani explains.

It contained the address, names, emails and phone numbers of residents and, more importantly, the skills and resources that people had – and the skills and resources that they might need. One of the resources one person needed was people to help him eat mulberries because, in the mulberry season, he had too many. It also meant that no one needed to buy a wheelbarrow – you could borrow one from Brian in number 33. And if you needed a trolley you could borrow it from Philip in number 29. And, of course, Obi at number 23 will babysit your cat.

The register revealed that three ladies would like to learn more about singing – and an ex-choir mistress also lived on the street – so, naturally, they formed the Hulbert Street Choir.

Patches of land around the street were planted with vegetables – and so the Hulbert Street Guerrilla Garden was created. Soon, it would not be uncommon for people to come home and find potatoes and carrots on their doorsteps. 'How did you get the permission?' people would ask Shani. 'Permission, do you think I need permission?' she would reply, and, based on that philosophy, the Hulbert Street Movies started – once a month, they would watch a movie together in the street. People brought their own chairs and a contribution to the pot-luck dinner.

The street-community resources grew to include a shared cargo bike, the Hulbert Street Book Exchange (bring a book, take a book) and a pizza oven on wheels (owned by no one yet shared by all), which led to weekly pizza dinners. And goats. Yes, goats. Two houses agreed to take down the fence between their lots and made room for them.

Shared pizza ovens and number of inter-front-lawn-goats are not a bad measure of the strength of a street community, but perhaps the best testimony were the reactions from the street when Shani and Tim had their safe, which held cash, a computer and back-up drives, stolen. Neighbours came by with food and money (one with a note: 'Here is $500. I am giving it because I can. Please do not give it back'). One neighbour started a Dropbox to help re-establish the files and pictures Shani and Tim had lost. One of the neighbours' sons gave them a card reading, 'Life's disappointments are harder to bear when you don't know any swear words' as he gave Shani the first loaf of bread he had ever baked and his entire collection of shells.

'What would you recommend people do if they want
to do what you did?' I asked Shani.

'Don't do anything we did,' she laughed. 'Figure out what works for
you. What to build your community around. Find out what interests
people, what unites people, and build on that. One of my friends
started to build a community in his street around tomatoes. Now
there are fifteen families coming together each year to can tomatoes.'

There are several things we can learn from Shani's story. First of all,
there is an advantage in being a defined community: Hulbert Street
is a cul-de-sac, which means the community is clearly geographically
defined. I suspect this is also one of the reasons why islanders often
experience a stronger sense of community and identity. Second, we
must seek to secure public space that can be used – a closed street
works because there is no through traffic, but so does a common piece
of green space. Third, one of the most powerful motivators is dreams.
Martin Luther King did not give an 'I have a nightmare' speech and,
in Hulbert Street, what sparked the community efforts was Shani's
question about what people would like to see their street be. Or, in
the words of Antoine de Saint-Exupéry, author of *The Little Prince*:

*'If you want to build a ship, don't drum up people
to collect wood and don't assign them tasks and
work, but rather teach them to long for the endless
immensity of the sea.'*

TAKE A STREET AND TURN IT INTO A COMMUNITY

Bring your local community together by creating a directory to share skills and resources.

Be like Shani and the community at Hulbert Street and start by building connections with your neighbours. Knocking on a neighbour's door for the first time may be terrifying for some, but the rewards can be big.

You could create a directory for the street or the stairway, ask whether they have some books they would like to donate for the mini-library you are setting up or whether they would like to take part in establishing a community garden in the neighbourhood.

The most important thing is to start talking with your neighbours, to learn their names, find out their skills, interests and needs and build a community around them – a community that is as unique as the people who live in your street.

IT TAKES A VILLAGE
TO RAISE HAPPINESS

▬▬▬▬▬▬

Think of a time when you felt happy or – feel free to tone it down a bit – a time you felt good, or laughed or smiled. Bring that memory to mind and try to remember the details of the situation.

Odds are you thought of a memory where you were together with other people. Mine is sitting in a cabin after a day of skiing, surrounded by friends, with a fire in the fireplace and whisky in my glass.

I have asked audiences across the world to think of good times and, more often than not, people are with other people in their memories. This proves nothing about the importance of people when it comes to happiness. However, people have an easier time remembering numbers and data if we give them some scenes to attach them to.

So, what does the evidence say? Well, if we look at the link with how often people meet socially with friends, colleagues or relatives, we see a clear pattern. The more often people meet, the happier they are. However, one thing is quantity, another thing is quality.

How often do you meet socially with friends, relatives or colleagues?

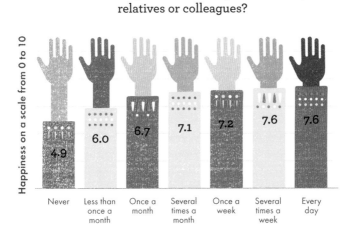

Happiness on a scale from 0 to 10

Never	Less than once a month	Once a month	Several times a month	Once a week	Several times a week	Every day
4.9	6.0	6.7	7.1	7.2	7.6	7.6

How many people are there with whom you can discuss intimate and personal matters?

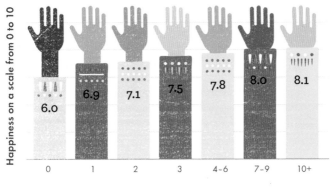

Happiness on a scale from 0 to 10

0	1	2	3	4-6	7-9	10+
6.0	6.9	7.1	7.5	7.8	8.0	8.1

Source: European Social Survey, 7th Wave

I cannot be the only one who has felt lonely in a crowded room. We may see and meet other people, but the important thing is whether we connect. Do I get you? Do you get me? Do you trust me enough to let your guard down, to let me know what is really on your mind? To let me in? We also see this reflected in the numbers. The more people we have with whom we can talk about personal matters, the happier we are.

So, loneliness is bad for happiness. Mind-blowing, right? More than two thousand years ago, Aristotle pointed out that man is a social animal; and, in the 1940s, Maslow's pyramid of human needs showed how love and belonging come just after basic safety and physiological needs.

Today, modern happiness research using big data echoes those findings. What the UN World Happiness Report shows us is that roughly three quarters of the difference in the happiness levels between the countries of the world comes down to six factors.

One of them is social support. We will look at the other five in the chapters to come. Social support is measured by asking whether people have somebody they can rely on in times of need. It is a binary and very crude way of measuring it, but we have data on it from around the globe, and it *does* determine happiness levels.

Fortunately, across the countries in the OECD (Organization for Economic Cooperation and Development), 88 per cent of people believe that they know someone they could rely on in a time of need. People in New Zealand, Iceland and Denmark feel most secure. In these countries, 95 per cent or above believe their friends have their back in times of need, while people in Hungary, Korea and Mexico report the lowest level of confidence with 82, 76 and 75 per cent, respectively.

A couple of years ago, I called my bank to see if I could borrow some money to buy a place to live. When I said that I studied happiness for a living, the man on the other end of the line went awfully quiet. Long story short, I was in my mid-thirties, single, and spent the next couple of months on my friend's couch with his two cats. You know, living the dream. But I didn't despair: I knew people had my back.

HAPPINESS TIP:
DO IT LIKE THE DUTCH - CELEBRATE NEIGHBOURS' DAY

Make the effort to speak to your neighbours. Meet them for a coffee, help them in the shared garden or just stop to chat the next time you see them.

According to a Dutch proverb, it is better to have a good neighbour than a distant friend. Since 2006, the Dutch have celebrated National Neighbours' Day on 26 May. It started as an initiative to get neighbours together and has grown to become an event which is celebrated in two thousand Dutch districts. It was inspired by a survey which showed that three out of four Dutch people found that neighbourhoods which engaged in regular activities were the most pleasant to live in and was initiated by the Dutch coffee company, Douwe Egberts, to get neighbours together. Later on, Douwe Egberts collaborated with the Oranjefonds, which has since 2008 provided neighbourhoods with funds to celebrate the annual day. Celebrations can range from holding a street party to having a cup of coffee with neighbours you might not usually socialize with. Make a special effort on 26 May next year to say hello to your neighbours, or invite them over for a hot drink.

BOWLING TOGETHER

Back in 2000, Harvard professor and political scientist Robert Putnam published Bowling Alone, *about the decline of American civil society. Putnam's diagnosis was that Americans were engaging less and less with their communities and this was damaging American society as a whole.*

Americans were far less likely to participate in voluntary work, to go to church, know their neighbours, invite friends home, go to bars, join unions or just spend time hanging out with friends (and their cats).

This is part of the reason why, over the past decades, countries like the US have become richer but have at the same time experienced a drop in happiness levels. Across the world, we seem to be looking for happiness in all the wrong places. To make matters worse, this is not a US thing but a global thing. We – human beings – are happier when we feel connected with others. And, so far, I have yet to discover a more powerful force to explain human happiness than the fulfilment of our longing for love, friendship and community. So, people want to belong, but they are not exactly sure how to make it happen.

This challenge has become even bigger with the advance of technology. We are connecting like never before, yet we still feel alone. Our relationships are complicated, they are demanding and they are messy – so we attempt to clean them up with technology. We prefer calling someone to meeting them in person – and would rather text than call. We are drawn in by the illusion of connection without the demands of intimacy, and while there are positive aspects of social media, for example, keeping in touch when geographically apart, we find that people who reduce their consumption of social media are happier and connect more in the *real* world.

In 2015, we ran an experiment at the Happiness Research Institute. We asked participants about different dimensions of happiness and then randomly allocated the participants either to a control group, which continued to use Facebook as usual, or a treatment group, which did not use Facebook for a week. When the week had passed, we asked the participants to evaluate their lives once more.

What we found was that the treatment group reported significantly higher levels of life satisfaction. The people in that group also reported higher levels of enjoyment in life and felt less lonely, and not using Facebook led to an increase in their social activity and their satisfaction with their social life. Further study is needed to understand the long-term effects of such an intervention but, for now, it is another piece of evidence demonstrating that, while digital technologies are still in their infancy, we, too, are still in our infancy in terms of our ability to use it. One of the challenges is to organize critical analogue mass at the local community level. By critical analogue mass, I mean enough people that are not sucked into their devices so there is someone to play or talk with. How do we ensure that we have somebody to play with if we disconnect from the digital community? As we shall see below, a Danish school might have found a means to do that.

HAPPINESS TIP:
CREATE CRITICAL ANALOGUE MASS

Encourage your friends and family to have tech-free periods during the week, avoid the temptation to check your phone, and detox digitally.

In addition to bonfires at summer solstice, the field across from our summer cabin was used for play. When I was a child, we could easily muster twenty-five kids for a game of roundball (best described as a simple version of baseball); of course, this was in the pre-iPad age. Last year, a survey from Action for Children in the UK showed that parents find convincing kids to turn off their computer, phone or other device tougher than getting them to do their homework. Almost one in four parents found it difficult to control the amount of time their children spent playing on computers or tablets, while only 10 per cent struggled with getting their children to do their homework. One of the reasons behind this is that kids do not want to be left out of the online community.

A Danish boarding school is going to what the kids consider extreme measures to create community. The staff confiscate smartphones and other gadgets; Facebook, Instagram and Snapchat can be accessed for only one hour per day, as pupils are allowed one hour of gadget time per day. After the first term, the system was put to a student vote. Should we continue with this system, or be given back our phones and gadgets and be free to use them as much as we want? Eighty per cent voted

for the first option. Obviously, these kinds of measures work only when a sufficient number of people are on board.

If you are the only one without your phone and the rest of the class is Snapchatting with their friends back home, that is a lonely experience. So it is important to get critical mass within your social circle. You could convince a number of families on your street to make Thursday night analogue night and send the kids out to play together, or start at home by making Thursday night family night. Other options are to create a no-phone zone for two hours around the evening meal, or place a basket for phones by the coat hangers and encourage friends to deposit any devices there when they visit.

TOGETHERNESS

Bofællesskab

Denmark: The co-housing scheme is designed to create privacy as well as community. Families live separately yet together, reducing social isolation and the hassle of everyday logistics. Read more on pp. 45–51.

Turning streets into communities

Perth, Australia: Using the wisdom of *The Little Prince*, Shani, a young Canadian woman, turned a street into a community by introducing pizza nights, movie nights, herb gardens and goats, through asking people to dream of what kind of street they would like to live in. Read more on pp. 57–63.

National Neighbours' Day

The Netherlands: The Dutch notion that a good neighbour is better than a distant friend has turned an initiative to get neighbours together over a cup of coffee into a nation-wide event that is celebrated in two thousand Dutch districts. Read more on p. 68.

From motor city to garden city

Detroit, USA: After the financial crisis which destroyed the economy in Detroit, people have started to revitalize the city by transforming it from a 'motor city' into a 'garden city'. Urban community gardens have been established throughout the city, which is currently one of the world's biggest urban agricultural movements.

Moai

Okinawa, Japan: Home to some of the healthiest people in the world, where many live to over a hundred years old. Some suggest it has to do with *moai*, which means to 'come together in a common purpose'. It is a solid part of Okinawan tradition to create small, secure social networks in which members commit to each other for life. *Moai* is created when a child is born and helps to integrate the child into a lifelong community. Whether you face serious problems in life, economic struggle, sickness or grief over the loss of a loved one, the *moai* will be there.

Día de los Muertos

Mexico: The Day of the Dead celebrations take place between 28 October and 2 November each year. The belief is that, on this day, the deceased have divine permission to visit friends and relatives on earth. People visit the graves of families and friends, taking food and drink with them. The events are a celebration of life rather than a sober mourning of its passing and create a sense of togetherness even with lost ones.

It takes a village to raise a child

Western Africa: The proverb 'It takes a village to raise a child' exists in many different African languages but is sometimes said to have originated in Igbo and Yoruba, which are spoken in Western Africa. Our language shapes our behaviour – and the proverb is a reminder that if we honour the notion that we are each other's keepers, we all become happier.

CHAPTER FOUR

———

MONEY

MONEY

*One day, when I was about eleven, I read the headline
'THE DOLLAR IS GOING TO RISE TO 8 KRONER IN A
YEAR' on the cover of* Børsen, *the Danish equivalent to
the* Financial Times.

At the time, the kroner was around 7 kroner to the dollar, so I did what
any normal kid would do, I went to the bank and had all my savings
converted to dollars.

'Are you going on holiday to the US?' the lady at the bank asked me, as
she was counting the money.

'No,' I said. 'Haven't you read *Børsen*?'

This was not an isolated incident. I bought my first bonds and stocks
when I was ten and had a poster in my room with a picture of a pile
of money on it and a caption that read 'My first million'. In school, my
class would participate in a mock stock-dealing game against other
classes, buying and selling stocks. However, as the prices we could
trade in were the prices in that day's paper, and therefore yesterday's
stock prices, I would call the bank every day to hear what the biggest
increases on the stock market had been and my class would buy that
stock. Grown-ups call that insider trading. We called it luck. In short, at
eleven, I was a pair of braces away from Gordon Gekko.

The reason why I am telling you all this is that, when you read the
following pages, you might think that I was some kind of hippie kid
who spent his days counting flowers. That was not the case. Oh, and
Børsen was wrong. The dollar dropped to 6 kroner. I still hold a grudge.

PEAK STUFF
FOR HAPPINESS

―――――――――

If money and happiness were to describe their relationship on Facebook, it would read: 'It's complicated.'

There is a correlation between income and happiness.

Generally speaking, in richer countries, people *are* happier. The gross domestic product – the GDP per capita, a nation's wealth – is one of the six factors that explain why people in some countries are happier than others.

However, it is important to emphasize that the connection is likely to be the fact that being *without* money is a cause of unhappiness. It makes sense to focus on improving material conditions in impoverished societies. Higher household income generally signifies an improvement in the living conditions of the poor – and, in turn, the happiness of the people.

So, when money means that we can put food on our table, have a roof over our head and support our children, money has the power to transform misery into happiness. But when money is spent on a $1,000 Serenity Dog Pod that lets your dog 'float away on a cloud-like bed into a blissful state with calming colour, changing light, relaxing and soothing music' (Google it; it's a thing), you have definitely run out of stuff you can buy that will improve your happiness. In fact, not only did you reach peak stuff for happiness a while back, but you fell off the cliff and now your dog is taking a dump on the summit.

Like most things, the more we have of something, the less happiness we derive from it. The first slice of cake: awesome. The fifth slice: not so good. Economists call this the law of diminishing marginal utility. That is one of the reasons why some countries and people get richer – but not happier. Another reason is that we adapt to new levels of wealth. In happiness research, we call this the hedonic treadmill.

GREAT EXPECTATIONS

We all daydream. I often imagine getting into shape, but then I realize it gets in the way of me levelling up in Candy Crush. *But we all do it. Daydream. Fantasize. Have great expectations about a future where we move to Paris, learn French and write a book.*

But how do our expectations and ambitions impact on our happiness? In order to create a better understanding of how ambition shapes our lives, Timothy Judge, professor of management at the University of Notre Dame's Mendoza College of Business, examined data that tracked the lives of 717 people. The data began in 1922 (the year a radio was first introduced into the White House) when the participants were children, and followed them for up to seventy years, a period during which the world lived through a World War, put a man on the moon, saw the rise and fall of empires – and the invention of the internet.

In the study, the participants were marked as more or less ambitious; this was based on self-assessment during the subject's youth and their parents' assessment. Perhaps unsurprisingly, the ambitious ones went on to be more successful in objective terms – going on to the more prestigious universities, such as Harvard and Princeton, working in more respected occupations and earning higher salaries.

In materialistic terms, Marcus Aurelius might have been right in saying that 'a man's worth is no greater than the worth of his ambitions', but perhaps he overlooked the fact that a man's worth does not equal his well-being.

For the ambitious among us, once we reach our goal we soon formulate another to pursue. This is the hedonic treadmill. We continuously raise the bar for what we want or feel we need in order to be happy – and the hedonic treadmill spins faster with ambition. In other words, the downside to being ambitious is a constant sense of dissatisfaction with our achievements.

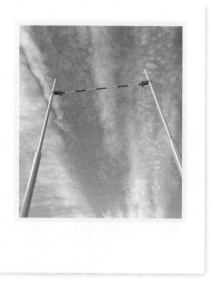

There might be some truth in the notion that happiness is ambition minus reality. So, could this be the reason why Danes score high on happiness? Is it because they have low expectations? Some have suggested as much.

One December around a decade ago, the *British Medical Journal* published an article called 'Why Danes are Smug: Comparative Study of Life Satisfaction in the European Union'. It concluded that the key factor in the high level of life satisfaction among the Danes was consistently low expectations for the year to come. 'Year after year, they are pleasantly surprised to find that not everything is getting more rotten in the state of Denmark.' This conclusion has been repeated by the BBC and CNN, among others. There is only one tiny issue: the article was meant as a joke.

The December issue was a Christmas edition which also featured explanations for why Rudolph has a red nose (apparently, it is due to a high density of capillaries in his nose); and the article about the happy Danes also looked at the impact of a high share of blondes living in the country, the level of beer consumption (a reviewer suggested that Danes were happy because they are drunk when they participate in the surveys), and concluded that another reason was that beating Germany 2–0 in the Euro 92 Championship football final put Denmark in such a state of euphoria that the country has not been the same since.

However, just because the article was built on humour rather than data does not mean that it might not be true.

Life satisfaction – now and in the future – among different income groups in Denmark

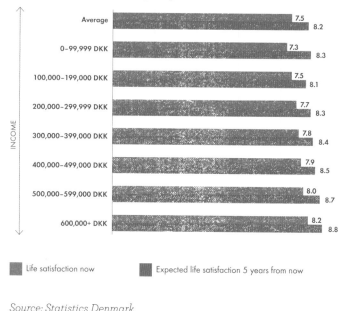

INCOME

	Now	Future
Average	7.5	8.2
0–99,999 DKK	7.3	8.3
100,000–199,000 DKK	7.5	8.1
200,000–299,999 DKK	7.7	8.3
300,000–399,000 DKK	7.8	8.4
400,000–499,000 DKK	7.9	8.5
500,000–599,000 DKK	8.0	8.7
600,000+ DKK	8.2	8.8

Life satisfaction now

Expected life satisfaction 5 years from now

Source: Statistics Denmark

Fortunately, data from Statistics Denmark can tell us whether this *is* true, because Statistics Denmark not only ask people how good they feel about their lives right now, they also ask how happy they imagine they will be five years from now – and Danes expect to be even happier in the future. So perhaps Danes are less ambitious when it comes to the accumulation of stuff – but I don't see any evidence that Danes have low expectations when it comes to happiness.

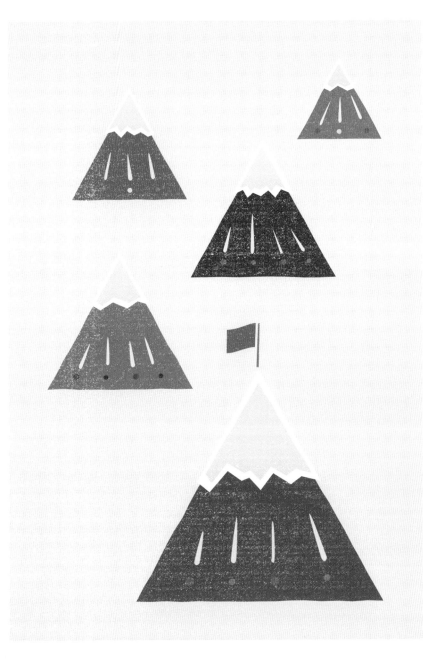

EXPECT THE HEDONIC TREADMILL

Take time to enjoy the journey towards your goal while also being mindful that achieving your goal will not fulfil you completely.

Expect and understand that reaching your goal might make you happy – but only for a while. We continuously raise the bar for what we want or feel we need in order to be happy. Getting your book published will make you happy for a while, and then you adjust your ambition to hitting the *Sunday Times* bestseller list, becoming a global phenomenon. I speak from personal experience.

I think we are yet to find the one thing that will permanently quench our thirst when it comes to ambition. So perhaps we need to consider how to turn the idea of the pursuit of happiness into the happiness of the pursuit. People on a quest for something they find meaningful – whether that is building a boat or growing the perfect tomato – tend to be happier; they know that happiness is the by-product of the process and not a pot of gold at the finish line.

EXPECTATION MAKES THE HEART GROW FONDER

―――――――――――

One morning, Winnie-the-Pooh and Piglet are talking about what they enjoy most in the world. And although Winnie is a big fan of eating honey, there is a moment just before he begins to eat which is better than eating itself, but he is not sure what it is called.

The A. A. Milne who wrote the stories about Winnie-the-Pooh was not an author, he was a happiness scientist. Expectation can be a source of joy. Imagine you could have a kiss from anyone you want. Any celebrity. Who would it be? George Clooney? Angelina Jolie? I would go with Rachel Weisz. (Yes, I know she is married to James Bond – no need to rub it in.) Do you have someone in mind? If you do, then consider this: When would you want that kiss? Now? In three hours? In twenty-four? In three days? In one year? In ten years?

If you are like the respondents in a study undertaken by George Loewenstein, professor in economics and psychology at Carnegie Mellon University and director of the Center for Behavioral Decision Research, you would want the kiss three days from now. Yes, someone actually researched this question.

The study, 'Anticipating and the Valuation of Delayed Consumption', was published in 1987 – the year of the release of *Dirty Dancing* – so now we know who all the respondents in the original study wanted to kiss. The study also showed that the respondents would be willing to pay more for the experience three days from now than for having the experience right now.

Every year, I prioritize a week of skiing in the Alps with my friends. Not only is it the purchase of an experience, it is also an investment in others – and something I look forward to for the half-year running up to it. Imagining my friends and me skiing down the mountain (me humming the James Bond theme), or relaxing on our balcony, with a sky that is the kind of blue that can only exist when it is paired with white, snow-covered mountains, I can already feel the warm cup of coffee in my hand and the sun on my face.

The point is, in some circumstances, expectation can be a source of great joy. However, we must also be aware that, in others, expectation and ambition can be a source of misery.

HAPPINESS TIP:
PAY NOW, CONSUME LATER

If you buy an experience, make sure that it is well into the future, so you can look forward to it.

Six months from now, what would you like to do? See a certain band with your friends? Invite someone who you feel a lot of gratitude towards to a nice restaurant? Buy the tickets or the gift certificate now. Or go long. Ten years from now, what would be your dream experience? Start putting money aside in a separate happiness account.

KEEPING UP WITH THE JONESES

When I do presentations I often ask the audience to imagine two worlds.

In the first world, you make £50,000 per year and everybody else makes £25,000. In the second world, you make £100,000 per year (so twice as much as before) and everybody else makes £200,000. Prices are constant, so a cup of coffee will cost the same in either world.

What about you? In which of these worlds would you choose to live? Usually, over 50 per cent of the audience would prefer to live in the first world. This is consistent with academic studies that have been carried out many times since the question was first posed at Harvard University in 1998. The reason why a large proportion of us prefer to live in the first world is that we not only care about our ability to consume, we also care about our position in the social hierarchy.

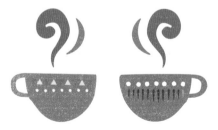

This is also the reason why we try to imitate the consumer pattern of people who are richer than we are. At the same time, the availability of credit has made it easier to imitate a lifestyle we cannot afford, and this, together with our desire to keep up with the Joneses, has been listed as one of the explanations for the financial crisis of 2008. In other words, we are spending money we don't have to buy stuff we don't need to impress people we don't like.

However, trying to signal that you have wealth is not a recent phenomenon. Back in 1899, the American sociologist Thorstein Veblen coined the term 'conspicuous consumption', which describes the phenomenon of buying luxury goods in order to publicly display your wealth to attain status. Veblen had noticed that a lot of the then nouveau riche Americans spent a great deal of their fortune on signalling how rich they were. This is the reason why some people today spend $15 million on a gold iPhone with six hundred inlaid white diamonds and fifty-three more diamonds for the Apple logo on the back. Apart from signalling how much money you have, it still does what a normal iPhone does and Siri still doesn't understand what you are saying. However, if you think that is extravagant, let me tell you that Aristotle Onassis had the bar stools on his luxury yacht, *Christina O*, upholstered with leather made from the foreskins of whales. So, if you ever feel bad about your indulgences, just remember that one of the world's richest men once spent a fortune on whale-foreskin bar stools.

The point of it all is that, if we spend our money on stuff we don't need to impress people, we are not getting closer to happiness, we are just getting involved in an arms race. That is why we would all be better off if we all put a lid on the bling.

You're not to think you are more important than we are.

You're not to think you are anything special.

You're not to convince yourself that you are better than we are.

You're not to think anyone cares about you.

THE LAW OF JANTE

In Denmark, and throughout the Nordic countries, conspicuous consumption is being somewhat curbed because of *Janteloven*, or the Law of Jante. The 'law' comes from a 1933 novel by Danish-Norwegian Aksel Sandemose and can be boiled down to 'You're no better than us.' It promotes a culture where people of high status are criticized because they have been classified as better – or pretend to be better – than their peers. In English, this is known as tall-poppy syndrome.

You're not to think you know more than we do.
You're not to think you are smarter than we are.
You're not to think you are good at anything.
You're not to think you are as good as we are.
You're not to laugh at us.
You're not to think you can teach us anything.

This is a big component of Scandinavian culture and the reason why you will see very few flashy luxury cars in Denmark. Well, that and a 150 per cent car tax, obviously. But the *Jantelov* goes deeper and wider than cars.

Where success may be enthusiastically flaunted in the US, humbleness is the bigger virtue in Scandinavia. Buy a luxury car with a personal licence plate saying 'SUCCESS' (as I saw in Riga, Latvia), and you can expect to have your car keyed within a day or two.

There are a lot of negative implications to the Law of Jante, but I do think we tend to overlook one positive aspect: it does seek to curb conspicuous consumption, and that may not be a bad thing. Being exposed to other people's wealth can have a negative effect. In South Korea, they have a saying for all this: 'If one cousin buys land, the other cousin gets a stomach ache.'

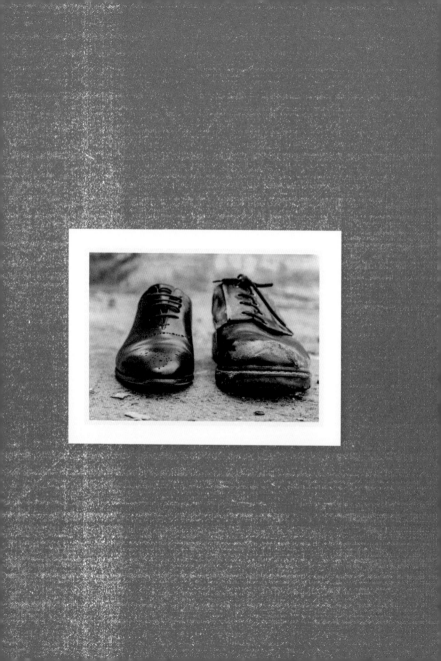

RICHER BUT NOT HAPPIER

In many ways, South Korea is the poster child for the key challenge facing many developed countries. Over the past two generations, South Korea has gone from being one of the poorest to one of the richest countries in the world.

While grandparents may remember famine, their grandsons and granddaughters enjoy some of the highest standards of living in the world, while the country holds top positions in life expectancy, health-care efficiency and proportion of people with a university education. The economic growth achieved by the South Korean people is quite simply an amazing achievement. Coming back to Copenhagen after visiting Seoul feels like travelling ten years back in time. However, the country is struggling to convert its new-found wealth into well-being. South Korea ranks fifty-fifth in the World Happiness Report of 2017 and, more alarmingly, it has top ranking when it comes to suicide rates in OECD countries.

South Korea also sends more visitors to our Happiness Research Institute than any other country. South Korean politicians, mayors, journalists, university students and professors have all come in search of ways to improve the quality of life in their country. 'For many years, we have been looking at the US as the big role model,' one told me. 'That is where we wanted to take the country. But now we are not so sure that's the way we wish to go any more.'

And the US is a key example when it comes to looking at how we have failed to transform wealth into well-being. While the US has achieved economic progress and an accumulation of wealth over the past half-century, this has not resulted in an increase of happiness for the people. One of the reasons for this is inequality. If a country doubles in wealth but 90 per cent of that wealth goes to the richest 10 per cent, that is not growth. That is greed. And no, Gordon Gekko, when it comes to happiness, greed is neither good, nor does it work. And your braces look stupid.

DECOUPLE WELL-BEING AND WEALTH

It is September, but it is still warm (from a Viking perspective) in Copenhagen, and this Friday there is a clear blue sky. I leave the office a bit earlier than usual and cycle ten minutes to the central harbour of Copenhagen to meet my buddy Michael for a swim.

Today, about a thousand overheated locals are splashing in the water of what used to be a corridor for heavy shipping traffic. The first harbour bath opened in Copenhagen in 2001, after the city invested in securing clean water, and there are now a handful of these urban oases in the centre of the city. This is during the period when I am living on my friend's couch. Money is tight but, fortunately, fun can be free.

In Copenhagen, I can cycle everywhere I need to go and so do not need money for fuel, or indeed a car. Regardless of how much I earn, the water will still be as clean and refreshing to swim in. Yes, of course money matters. Eating at the restaurant Noma may still be reserved for the few, but the Nordic countries have managed to some extent to decouple wealth from well-being for the individual.

I think what works well in Denmark is that enjoying a good quality of life does not have to cost a lot of money. If I lost my job and my savings, I would still be able to enjoy most of the same things I enjoy today.

Well, that is easy for you to say, I hear you cry. Try cycling in London – you'd be killed. That is very likely (it is the driving-on-the-opposite-side thing). Therefore, I think it is interesting to hear the story of Michelle McGagh, who went a year without spending a single pound. Michelle is a freelance journalist from north London and the woman behind the book *The No Spend Year: How I Spent Less and Lived More*.

CASE STUDY
MICHELLE

In 2015, Michelle McGagh found herself stuck in a cycle of consumerism – earning money to buy stuff she didn't really need. She felt lured by advertisements promising that she could spend her way to happiness.

So, she decided to give herself the challenge of not buying anything she didn't absolutely need for 365 days. What she would spend money on was the mortgage, essential bills such as utilities, including phone and internet (as she was working as a journalist), and basic groceries (£30 a week).

'It wasn't easy,' she tells me – especially starting the challenge in a dark and cold November. At this time of year, her life would usually revolve around going to pubs and restaurants, and now she couldn't. 'I was trying to do what I always did, but now I didn't have money to do it, so it didn't work and I felt a bit miserable.'

With spring came a big difference. It became more fun to go for walks and bike rides, and even to swim in lakes, and easier to explore London and seek out free art exhibitions and museums. She used sites like Eventbrite to find free film screenings, wine tastings and theatre productions.

'I've definitely gone to more art exhibitions than ever before – my favourite being First Thursdays, where 150 galleries in east London open late.'

The challenge taught Michelle to be more adventurous. 'I had to learn new ways to find happiness, so I ended up saying yes to things I definitely wouldn't have said yes to before. I pushed myself to my limits, and I realized that I don't need stuff to be happy.' She even had a free holiday, cycling along the British coast and camping on beaches. 'It's something I'd never done before, and probably wouldn't have, were it not for the challenge – and now I can't wait to go again next year.'

The ancient Greek stoic and philosopher Epictetus once said that wealth consists not in having great possessions but in having few wants. And while Michelle's challenge may be too extreme for many, we could all consider how we might decouple happiness from wealth. When we discover that our happiness does not rest on the foundation of money, we have found a true treasure.

Save big purchases until a noteworthy occasion, so that the item is worth so much more than what is on the price tag because it embodies your memory of that time.

If you must buy things, try to link them with a happy milestone, memory or experience. For example, I saved money for a new chair but waited until I had published my first book to buy it. Or look for things that will bring you happy moments in the future. Consider how a purchase will affect your behaviour in time to come.

A few years ago, the Happiness Research Institute was working with a town in Denmark on how to improve well-being for the children in state schools. One of our recommendations was that the town should invest in having an apple tree for each pupil in their schools: 7,439 children equals 7,439 trees. When a child started at the school, they would be shown their tree. During the harvest, each class would get together to pick the apples. And, on the last day of school, the children would hand over their tree to a new pupil who was just starting.

As well as teaching the children something about where food comes from, enjoying simple pleasures like watching the apples grow and eating them, working together as a group to harvest them, the pride and responsibility that comes from taking care of a tree and handing it on to a new generation, I thought this was a great investment for the schools. The town council thought otherwise. So, some town somewhere can still choose to be the first that grants every child an apple tree. Surely someone must be interested in being the town that ensures every child has at least one happy memory of picking apples.

THREE INEXPENSIVE ATTITUDES THAT CAN BRING HAPPINESS

1. READING

Reading – especially if you use the public library or the mini-library you have established in your stairway – is free. To me, the perfect afternoon is a book and a blanket in the shade of a tree on a summer's day – and since you are reading this, you probably already agree. Bibliotherapy, the art of using books to aid people in solving the issues they are facing, has been around for decades, and the belief in the healing power of books is said to go as far back as ancient Egypt and Greece, where signs above libraries would let readers know that they were entering a healing place for the soul. More recently, psychologists at the New School for Social Research found that fiction books improve our ability to register and read others' emotions and, according to an article in the *Journal of Applied Social Psychology*, research also shows that literary fiction enhances our ability to reflect on our problems through reading about characters who are facing similar issues and problems. Basically, reading is free therapy.

2. CREATE A SMILE FILE

Ruby Receptionist has been named the number-one small company to work for in the US by *Fortune* magazine. When a new employee starts there, they are handed a 'Smile File' and asked to write down every nice comment they receive from co-workers, clients and their bosses. Why? Because people remember criticism far better than praise. It is an inexpensive approach we can apply in our personal lives to become more aware of the things that we *do* have, instead of focusing on what we *don't*. Once a week, write down three to five things you are grateful for. Anything from 'My family and friends are healthy' to 'Coffee and the Rolling Stones', but try also to elaborate on how they impact on your life in a positive way. Studies show that translating our thoughts into concrete written language has advantages, compared to just thinking about it. It makes us more aware and increases the emotional impact. In recent years, 'gratitude journals' have become more and more popular, but it is important not to treat these exercises as just another item on your to-do list. Also, studies show that it is better to do it occasionally – say, once a week – than every day, to keep it from becoming a routine.

3. ESTABLISH A FREE-FUN FELLOWSHIP

Like Michelle used to before taking on the challenge of the no-spend year, many of us organize our social life around restaurant visits or bars. If money becomes tight, you may risk becoming isolated. In order to counter that, you might form a free-fun fellowship in which each friend takes a turn at planning an inexpensive activity and you all meet up to spend time together doing it.

What my fellowship has done is to watch the horse races (bring a pot-luck picnic), visit museums, go swimming, play board games and go hiking in Dyrehaven (the king's former hunting grounds north of Copenhagen, where you can see hundreds of deer). These things might not be for you. You may hate deer and trees, and you may have to find your own way, but the point is to try to remove the value and power of money when it comes to happiness.

HAPPINESS – WHERE TO GET BANG FOR YOUR BUCK

As a group, on average, the richer countries are happier, but if we zoom in on the richest countries in the world, we don't see a clear pattern.

Qatar, the richest country in the world, ranks thirty-fifth in the 2017 World Happiness Report, while a poorer country, Costa Rica, ranks twelfth. And some countries seem to be better at converting wealth into well-being for their people. For instance, the US is the eighteenth richest country in the world, with a GDP higher per capita than Denmark, Finland, Sweden and Iceland, but reports lower levels of happiness than all these countries.

This demonstrates two things. First, while money matters, it is not all that matters. Second, it is not only about how much money we make, it is also about what we do with the money we have. The most successful countries in the twenty-first century will be those that most efficiently turn wealth into well-being – and this also applies to the individual. So how do we get most bang for our buck when it comes to happiness?

BUY MEMORIES, NOT THINGS

'Now you have earned your name. You are a proper Viking now.'

These words are from Jussi, my publisher in Finland. It was early January and I had just risen from the freezing waters of Helsinki. It was the first time I had tried winter swimming and, earlier that day, I had googled 'Can you die from ice swimming?' So much for being a brave Viking.

Before we jumped into the dark, icy water, we spent an hour in a beautiful wooden public sauna by the harbour in Helsinki. As soon as Jussi had picked me up from the airport, our conversation steered towards the unique sauna culture of Finland.

'Finnish saunas are better than Swedish saunas.'

'How are they better?' I asked, not being sure how you would judge the quality of a sauna.

'They are warmer.'

'Warmer' was an understatement. Every breath I took in the sauna I felt like I was inhaling a chilli, and I discovered that I have the ability to sweat inside my mouth. Admittedly, not one of the cooler superhero powers but, at that time, it proved very useful.

Every twenty minutes, one of the Finns operating the sauna would enter, pose a question, and the Finnish men and women in there would say, *kyllä*, the Finnish word for 'yes'. You could recognize every non-Finn in the room. Not by the fact that they were not saying *kyllä*, but by the sheer look of panic as they thought, Oh my God, did he just ask if we wanted the sauna to be warmer?, followed by the operator pouring water over the heated rocks and causing more hot steam to fill the room and our lungs.

Nevertheless, being exposed to the extreme heat in a dark room forces you to concentrate on your breathing, and it was a wonderful and meditative experience. One of the first things I did when I came back to Copenhagen was to look for saunas. Furthermore, on that day in Helsinki, the intense heat converted my fear of the icy-cold water awaiting me into a feeling of pleasant anticipation. It was cold, yes, but it was not the near-death experience I had imagined. The feeling of being alive and experiencing my body warm, despite standing semi-naked in the dark Helsinki night in January after swimming among ice, was pure joy. The whole experience might only have taken a couple of hours, but it is a memory I will carry with me for ever.

HAPPINESS TIP: BUY EXPERIENCES

Buy experiences and memories, not things.

According to researchers Dunn and Norton, if we are looking to buy happiness, it is wiser to invest in experiences rather than things, as 'study after study [shows that] people are in a better mood when they reflect on their experiential purchases which they describe as "money well spent"'. If people are asked to compare purchases they made with the intent of increasing their happiness – one where they bought something tangible (like an iPhone, gold-plated or not) and one where they bought an experience (a trip, maybe) – and are then asked which purchase made them happier, 57 per cent will say the experience compared to 34 per cent the tangible object.

Buying experiences is especially good for happiness if these experiences bring you together with other people and if they are linked with who you see yourself as being. As an example, I see myself as a happiness researcher, therefore I may get more pleasure out of visiting Bhutan – the country that has instituted policies based on gross national happiness since the 1970s – than you. See experiences as an investment in happy memories and in your personal story and development.

BUY MEANINGFUL EXPERIENCES
THAT ARE PART OF SOMETHING
BIGGER

*Try also to buy experiences that can be part of a
bigger journey for you. Something that takes you
closer to a lifelong passion. For instance, why not
become the world's leading expert in blue?*

You would have to look into history (why do we call
royal blood blue blood?), science (why is the sky blue?),
anthropology (what are the different cultural connotations
of blue?), language (why are blue, *blau* (German) and *bleu*
(French) similar, but so different to *azul* (Spanish), *niebieski*
(Polish) and *sininen* (Finnish)?), anatomy (how many shades
of blue can the human eye identify?), genetics (why do so few
people have blue eyes?) and photography (what is so magical
about the blue hour?).

If you were to become the expert in blue, imagine saving up
for and planning to visit Chefchaouen, the completely blue
city in the Rif mountains of northern Morocco, the Blue Nile
in Ethiopia, or the Blue Mountains in Australia, where an
organic chemical found in the abundant eucalyptus trees in
the mountains provides elements for the blue haze after which
the mountains were named. Those experiences would be even
more rewarding if they were part of your passion for blue.

It would also provide you with an identity beyond your job.
So what do you do? I am interested in the colour blue.

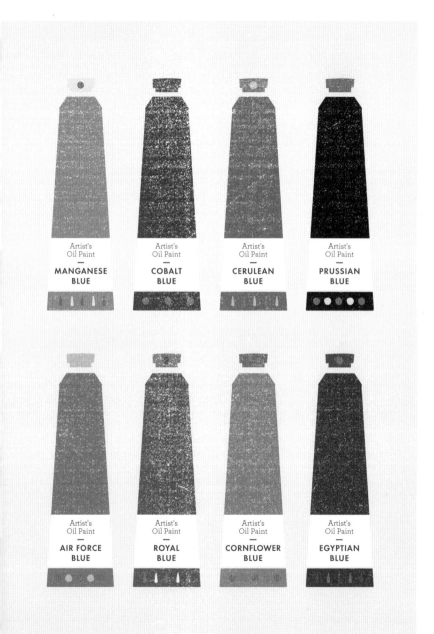

Artist's
Oil Paint
—
**MANGANESE
BLUE**

Artist's
Oil Paint
—
**COBALT
BLUE**

Artist's
Oil Paint
—
**CERULEAN
BLUE**

Artist's
Oil Paint
—
**PRUSSIAN
BLUE**

Artist's
Oil Paint
—
**AIR FORCE
BLUE**

Artist's
Oil Paint
—
**ROYAL
BLUE**

Artist's
Oil Paint
—
**CORNFLOWER
BLUE**

Artist's
Oil Paint
—
**EGYPTIAN
BLUE**

HOW MUCH MONEY
DOES HAPPINESS BUY?

———————

*Finally, when it comes to money and happiness,
while money may reduce misery and thus cause higher
levels of life satisfaction, the reverse relationship –
that happiness may lead to a higher income – may also
be true.*

At least, that is what Dr Jan-Emmanuel De Neve and Professor
Andrew Oswald have found. Jan-Emmanuel is associate professor of
economics and strategy at Said Business School and the University
of Oxford – but, more importantly, a nice guy. I met him the first
time in the United Arab Emirates at a conference on happiness.

'We have been looking at the graphs the wrong way,' says Jan. 'We
present the data like happiness is the function of income – but what
if we got it wrong? What if the relationship goes the other way?'

'You would need to follow thousands of people over decades to
prove that.'

'We proved it. We used the Add Health Data.' Add Health Data
is a large US sample of representative individuals who have
been studied over time, and includes data on positive affect, life
satisfaction and income.

'Their happiness level when they are young predicts their income later in life.'

'But could it be that parents with longer education and higher income have happier kids, and those parents also make sure that kids go to university and therefore end up with higher income later in life?' I ask, and feel quite proud, as I am by far the dumbest guy at the table.

'Here is the kicker,' Jan says, smiling and leaning in over the table, as if he is about to reveal the nuclear launch codes. 'We have thousands of siblings in the study – so we can remove the effect of the parents. The happier brother is going to make more money later in life.'

And the effect is big. The study shows that a one-point increase in happiness on a five-point scale at the age of twenty-two means an income higher by $2,000 seven years later. Positive people seem more likely to get a degree, find a job and be promoted. In addition, the study's results are robust and include controls such as education, IQ, physical health, height, self-esteem and later happiness.

The implication of this study underlines the importance of the subjective well-being of our kids – and I also understand why Jan lowered his voice when he revealed their findings. The knowledge would be dangerous in the hands of kids. 'No need to do homework, Dad. Just give me some sweets – otherwise my future earnings may be in jeopardy.' Let's keep the study 'Estimating the Influence of Life Satisfaction and Positive Affect on Later Income Using Sibling Fixed-Effects' to ourselves, shall we?

MONEY

Investing in the common good

The Nordic countries: Wide public support for a high level of taxation means a good return on quality of life. Read more on p. 42.

The 'spend less, live more' experiment

UK: As an experiment, Michelle McGagh spent one year buying the bare minimum and found ways to enjoy life without financial wealth. Read more on pp. 102–104.

The Giving Pledge

US: The Giving Pledge is a philanthropic initiative started by Warren Buffett and Bill and Melinda Gates which encourages the world's wealthiest individuals and families to donate the majority of their wealth to help address society's biggest issues, from the alleviation of poverty to health care to education. Today, more than 150 billionaires from more than fifteen countries have signed the pledge.

Targeting the Ultra-poor Programme

Pabna, Bangladesh: The development organization BRAC helps people out of poverty by bringing them together and having them pool their resources to start their own businesses and to resolve problems in the community.

The Robin Hood Restaurant

Madrid, Spain: Established by the charity Mensajeros de la Paz, this is a typical restaurant by day but, at night, it transforms into a pioneering place where homeless people can dine at tables set with flowers and with proper cutlery and glasses, free of charge. The restaurant uses the money from the paying customers at breakfast and lunch to fund these free evening meals.

Reaching Out Vietnam

Hoi An, Vietnam: Reaching Out Vietnam provides opportunities for people of disability to learn skills and gain meaningful employment so that they are able to integrate fully into their communities and lead independent and fulfilling lives. Fairtrade giftshops sell items made by disabled people in Vietnam and the profits are fed back into the business to assist disabled people by giving them training and finding them jobs.

CHAPTER FIVE

—

HEALTH

HEALTH

―――――――――
―――――――――

Across cultures, there seems to be one thing that all parents wish for their children: good health. Good health enables us to play, to seek out adventures, to pursue happiness.

At the Happiness Research Institute, we, together with Leo Innovation Lab, have explored how psoriasis – a chronic and recurrent inflammatory disease of the skin – affects happiness. Up to the time of writing, the PsoHappy project has collected data from almost fifty thousand people from more than forty countries across the world. In every country, we find that those living with psoriasis are less happy than the general population.

As a happiness researcher, I cannot see a more obvious policy to improve quality of life than by providing universal health care. In the Nordic countries, all of which consistently rank among the ten happiest countries in the world, free health care is available to everyone. People simply have less to worry about in daily life than most other people on this front, and that forms a sound basis for high levels of happiness.

Or, as US senator Bernie Sanders puts it,

'In Denmark, there is a very different understanding of what "freedom" means. In that country, they have gone a long way to ending the enormous anxieties that come with economic insecurity. Instead of promoting a system which allows a few to have enormous wealth, they have developed a system which guarantees a strong minimal standard of living to all – including the children, the elderly and the disabled.' In other words, *Breaking Bad*, the TV drama where a teacher turns drug lord to pay his medical bills for cancer treatment, would have made a pretty shitty TV show in a Nordic context. 'Here is your treatment plan, Walter. I will see you on the fifth.'

Furthermore, there is a reverse relationship between happiness and health: our happiness has an impact on our health. A greater level of happiness predicts better future physical health. According to the World Happiness Report 2012:

> *The medical literature has found high correlations between various low well-being scores and subsequent coronary heart disease, strokes and length of life. Individuals with higher positive affect have better neuroendocrine, inflammatory and cardiovascular activity. Those with higher positive affect are less likely to catch a cold when exposed to a cold virus and recover faster if they do.*

One example of these studies was conducted by Andrew Steptoe, professor of psychology and head of the research department of Behavioural Science and Health at the Institute of Epidemiology and Health Care at University College London (UCL), and Jane Wardle, professor in clinical psychology at the Health Behaviour Research Centre, also at UCL. Over a five-year period, they conducted a survey of the participants' affective happiness, following about four thousand Brits aged between fifty-two and seventy-nine years old, divided into three groups, and asking them about their mood. It turned out that the happiest third had a 34 per cent lower mortality rate – even after controls undertaken for demographics and health status at the outset.

Life Expectancy in Years

Japan	83.7
Switzerland	83.4
Singapore	83.1
Australia	82.8
Spain	82.8
Iceland	82.7
Italy	82.7
Israel	82.6
Sweden	82.4
France	82.4
Norway	81.8
United Kingdom	81.2
Finland	81.1
Portugal	81.1
Germany	81
Denmark	80.6
United States	79.3
Poland	77.5
Brazil	75
Russian Federation	70.5
India	68.5
Sierra Leone	50.1

Source: World Health Organization

Going by this, you would expect that the happy Danes enjoy the world's longest life expectancy. But that is not the case. That honour goes to Japan. Denmark comes in at twenty-seventh, with Danes living a little over a year longer than the Americans but half a year less than the British. In addition, of all the Nordic populations, Danes live the shortest time.

In general, Danes smoke a lot, drink a lot and eat loads of meat and sugar, which is not compatible with a long and healthy life. *Hygge* – the cornerstone of Danish culture and the Danish way of life – is, in part, about indulging in cinnamon swirls and hot chocolate with whipped cream without ordering a side of guilt. *Hygge* may be good for happiness, but it is not necessarily good for health.

Last year, *hygge* became such a global phenomenon that it drove up demand for baked goods and affected the global spice market. 'Since *hygge* took off, we've been selling a third more cakes and buns,' Jonas Aurell from ScandiKitchen in London told the *Financial Times*. Meanwhile, the price of cinnamon swirled upwards by 20 per cent.

Of course, that raised the question, if the Danes binge on baked goods like the Fraggles down doozer sticks, why does Denmark rank 107th when it comes to obesity (compared with the UK at 43rd place and the US at 18th)?

Danes balance the cinnamon swirls with physical activity. Not every Dane is a fjord-swimming, cycling, cross-country-skiing aficionado, but 31 per cent of Danes are physically active at least five hours per week in their spare time, according to Eurostat, the EU's statistical office. But Danes dislike the gym every bit as much as everyone else, so how do they get so much exercise?

TWO-WHEELED VIKINGS

Be careful when you walk the streets of Copenhagen for the first time. Walking on a cycle path in the Danish capital prompts the same reaction from locals as picnicking on the path for the Bull Run would during San Fermin in Pamplona.

In Copenhagen, 45 per cent of all commutes for work or education are by bike. If we look at the people working *and* living in Copenhagen, the number rises to 63 per cent of commutes. Oh, and most of them are not colourful 'MAMILs' (middle-aged men in Lycra). You are just cycling to work; it's not the Tour de France. People wear stilettos, suits . . . and, last New Year's Eve, I even cycled in my smoking jacket.

THE TWO-WHEELED TAKEOVER

The two-wheeled takeover of Copenhagen is quite a recent development. There are now more bikes than cars in the heart of the city. In fact, it seems the only thing more abundant than cyclists here is statistics about bikes. According to the Cycling Embassy of Denmark (yes, that is a thing):

Nine out of ten Danes own a bicycle

There are five times as many bikes as cars in Copenhagen

63 per cent of all members of the Danish Parliament cycle to work daily

58 per cent of children cycle to school in Copenhagen – the national average is 44 per cent of all children aged between ten and sixteen

Copenhagen has more than 450 kilometres of bike paths

17 per cent of all trips in Denmark are made by bike (however, the share is much higher in concentrated urban areas like Copenhagen)

17 per cent of all families with kids have a cargo bike

On average, Danes cycle 1.5 km a day

18,000 bikes are stolen every year in Copenhagen

75 per cent of cyclists cycle all year round

The cyclists of Copenhagen cycle more than 1.2 million kilometres every day

Nowhere are these statistics more evident than during the morning rush hour on Nørrebrogade – Copenhagen's busiest bike corridor. That was my commute for about eight years, and I was joined every morning by students, businessmen and businesswomen, members of parliament and toddlers in training.

The reasons for the hordes of Vikings on two wheels are the good conditions provided for cyclists. If you visit Copenhagen, it's easy to spot the lengths the city goes to to make them happy. There are tilted bins (so you can get rid of your to-go coffee cup while cycling at speed without missing the bin), footrests for cyclists when they are waiting at traffic lights – and if there has been a snowfall, bicycle lanes are cleared before those for cars.

Cyclists here are not treated like second-class citizens; they are treated not only with dignity but as kings and queens of the road.

HAPPINESS TIP:
GET ON YOUR BIKE

This weekend, dust off your bike and get outside.

You may have fond childhood memories of riding around on your bike. It was fun, right? It is time to rekindle that love – or maybe it's time for you to fall in love with two wheels for the first time. If you've never tried cycling before, find a school or someone to teach you. If you have no bike, borrow one – or maybe you live in a city with a bike-sharing scheme. Figure out a way you can substitute driving or passive transportation with going by bike – or just go for a weekend tour by the beach, in the park, anywhere.

EXTENDING
YOUR LIFE*CYCLE*

───────

Our body mass index (BMI) is not a satisfactory measure of health, and, obviously, our health is about more than our weight – but here is the best news when it comes to cycling.

A new study by the University of Glasgow published in the *British Medical Journal* in 2017 found that cycling to work is associated with a 41 per cent lower risk of premature death, compared with a non-active commute to work. For instance, people who cycle to work have a 45 per cent lower risk of developing cancer and a 46 per cent lower risk of heart disease. The research is rigorous and used data from more than 260,000 participants in the UK Biobank, following them for five years. The new cases of cancer, heart attacks and deaths in that five-year period were assessed and cross-referenced to the participants' mode of commuting. The results of this study are consistent with what Danish studies have discovered about the health benefits of cycling.

One of these studied more than fifty thousand Danes between the ages of fifty and sixty-five. The participants were followed for twenty years; those who didn't cycle to work when the study began but started doing so in the first five years of the study had a 26 per cent lower risk of developing heart disease, compared to the passive commuters. Which goes to show that it's never too late to take up healthy habits. Another Danish study found that the mortality rate is 30 per cent lower for people who commute by bike, compared to passive commuters.

In addition, cycling has been shown to have a preventative effect on non-insulin-dependent diabetes, osteoporosis and depression. The British Medical Association found that the increased life expectancy gained from exercise via cycling outweighs the added risk incurred from accidents by a factor of twenty. Of course, accidents happen, but for every cyclist casualty in Copenhagen, cyclists have biked 4.4 million kilometres – the equivalent of 110 times around the world. Cycling keeps us more active and healthier, which in turn keeps us happier – in both the short and the long run.

In addition to adding years to our lives and reducing our waistlines, bikes also reduce congestion, air pollution and noise and improve the bottom line of our cities financially. The municipality of Copenhagen has examined the effects of travelling by bike and car. Looking at the total cost of air pollution, accidents, congestion, noise and wear and tear on infrastructure when travelling by each method, bikes save the city 0.45 kroner (about 5 pence) for every kilometre travelled, compared to travelling by car. With over 400 million kilometres cycled every year in the capital, it adds up.

Nor is it a coincidence that, among the cities competing for the title of most liveable city in the world in rankings by *Monocle* and *Mercer*, most of them are also among the most bikeable cities. As well as Copenhagen, cities such as Berlin, Vienna and Stockholm fall into this category. Two thirds of all citizens in Copenhagen believe that bikes have a positive or very positive impact on the city's atmosphere.

However, for most Danes, none of this matters. The primary reason for us to cycle is not to make ourselves healthier, our cities less congested, our economy stronger or our planet more sustainable – we do it simply because it is easy and convenient.

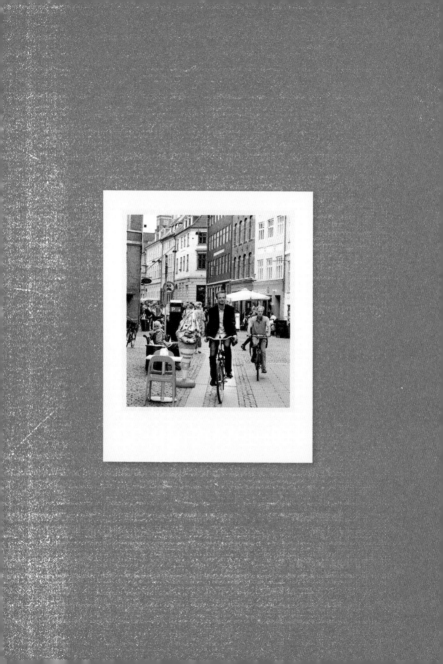

OUTDOING THE DANES

'A city is successful not when it's rich but when its people are happy. Creating bikeability and walkability shows respect for human dignity. We're telling people, "You are important – not because you're rich, but because you are human." If people are treated as special, as sacred, even, they behave that way. We need to walk just as birds need to fly. Creating public spaces is one way to lead us to a society that is not only more equal but also much happier.'

The words are those of Guillermo Peñalosa, who I met at a conference in Kuala Lumpur. He is the former Commissioner of Parks, Sport and Recreation for the City of Bogotá, Colombia. I recognized the passionate speech about walkability from something I heard a few years earlier from a man with the same surname.

'Are you by any chance related to Enrique Peñalosa?' I asked. Guillermo stretched out his arms and smiled: 'He is my brother.' Enrique is the mayor of Bogotá, and the brothers have a passion for walking, cycling and public spaces that puts even people from Copenhagen to shame.

The biggest obstacles to happiness are feeling inferior or excluded. A good city does not let its citizens feel this way. The same day I met Gil, I had tried to walk to a botanical garden two hundred metres from the conference venue, but gave up, as there were no pavements that could take me there.

'A developed country is not a place where the poor have cars. It's where the rich use public transport. It is where the rich walk and where they use bikes. We should create cities where rich and poor meet as equals: in parks, on the pavements, on public transport.'

His point is that great public spaces – like beautiful parks, bike paths and walkable streets – function as social blenders; as equalizers in our cities and societies. We usually meet under the same conditions of social hierarchy. At work, you are the boss or the employee. At the restaurant, you are being served or serving others.

One of the initiatives to have come out of Bogotá is Ciclovía, in which the city closes off more than a hundred kilometres of streets to car traffic on Sundays. Instead, the streets are converted to walkable, bikeable and playable areas; more than a million people make use of this. This initiative has spread to more cities throughout the world and is one small step towards us getting more exercise into our daily lives.

WALK MORE

Here are ten ways to get more exercise
without hitting the gym and, at the same time,
meet more people in your community:

1. Say no to escalators.

2. Walk over and talk to a colleague instead of calling or emailing.

3. Find a walk buddy. A walking partner can be a strong incentive to walk daily, especially when the sky is grey or you find another excuse not to.

4. Take the scenic route. There are apps (try Kamino and Field Trip) that will tell you not the fastest route but the prettiest.

5. Make Wednesdays Walking Wednesdays: a day when your family, friends or just you go for an after-dinner stroll.

10. Join a walking group or a hiking club. There might already be a walking group in your neighbourhood – if not, ask your neighbours if they are interested in forming one.

9. Meet your friends for a walk, not a coffee – or just have the coffee while you're walking.

8. Walk, don't wait. If you arrive early for an appointment – at the doctor's, for example – take a walk around the block rather than simply sitting in the waiting room.

7. Bring a podcast. If you are by yourself, you can also listen to one of the many great free ones. My favourites are RadioLab and This American Life.

6. Go on a coin-flip safari. This is a great way to get to see new parts of your neighbourhood. We tend to walk the same routes when we go for a stroll so, next time, take a coin with you and, at every junction, let the coin decide where you go. Getting to know your neighbourhood better will make you feel even more at home there, and you might discover new places where you love to go.

HAPPINESS TIP:
MOVE MORE EACH DAY

Build more movement into your daily routine: take the stairs, have a meeting while going for a walk and park as far away from the supermarket entrance as possible.

The obvious tip here would be to start biking to work, or school, or anywhere. However, your city may not be ready for cycles, so getting your local city council to start investing in infrastructure for people, not cars, could be the first step on a long road. However, there are also some short-term solutions.

The reason why Danes exercise more than everybody in the EU is that they don't see it as exercise. They see it as transportation. A small dose of fitness becomes part of your normal life instead of something you do in the gym.

This runs against the fact that we have built overly convenient societies – we sit still at work, we stand still on the escalator, we walk through doors that open automatically, we take the lift, we drive to the gym to train on the Stairmaster for an hour. So, I think the key lesson from the Danish way of living when it comes to health is to build movement into your daily routine.

The Happiness Research Institute is located by the lakes of central Copenhagen. On our side, there is no traffic and thus no noise, which allows me to walk by the lakes when I need to make a long phone call, and even to convert some meetings into walk'n'talks – for instance, my employees and I have monthly conversations instead of yearly reviews, and these are done while we walk.

Moreover, when I ask our barista for a cup of coffee, I then walk five floors up to the top of the building and back down again, and the coffee is ready. It doesn't take any more time and, as I drink four cups a day, it means I climb the stairs of a hundred-storey building every week. Similarly, every two hours in front of the computer 'costs' twenty-five push-ups.

Do I get embarrassed when colleagues catch me doing this?

Totally.

Do I believe it is worth the embarrassment?

I do.

MOOD BOOSTERS

———————

The Danish love of bicycles comes partly from their effect on our everyday mood. Apart from the exercise that comes from walking or cycling rather than driving, studies show that both cycling and walking put us in a better mood than driving.

A group of scientists at McGill University in Montreal has looked into which sort of transport is best for our mood. The study was conducted among 3,400 people – during summer and winter – and examined six typical means of transport: car, bus, train, metro, bicycle and foot. The researchers looked at the satisfaction gained in several aspects of the journeys and from this calculated one overall satisfaction score for each mode of transport. They found that the greatest satisfaction was experienced by those who could walk to work, while those who had to take the bus were the least satisfied.

Obviously, you might say. If you can walk to work, you can't have a three-hour commute. That is true: the length of the commute does dictate our transport options somewhat. So, it's particularly interesting to study commuters over time and observe what happens when they change their form of transport.

Fortunately, that is exactly what scientists from the universities of East Anglia and York have done, by following a group of eighteen thousand Britons over eighteen years in the 2014 study 'Does Active Commuting Improve Psychological Well-being? Longitudinal Evidence from Eighteen Waves of the British Household Panel Survey' (the rule of thumb in academic papers being, the longer the title, the better). They found that people who switched from driving to walking or cycling experienced improvements in psychological well-being – even if the trip now took *longer*.

I cycle to work and pass a large public garden on my way. The garden is one of the ways I can sense that spring is coming: I can smell when the cherry trees are blooming. Part of the reason why we feel in a better mood when cycling rather than driving is that our senses are more engaged. We simply feel more alive – walking is a more sensual experience than driving. Especially if you engage in what the Japanese call *shinrin-yoku*.

AS EASY AS A WALK
IN THE . . . FOREST

▬▬▬▬▬

You take a long, deep breath and your lungs fill up with the moist, fresh air. The leaves are the colour that only the first weeks of spring bring and the sun's rays dance off them as you slowly make your way through the forest.

As you pause for a moment and close your eyes, the only sounds you can hear are your breath, a distant bird and the wind in the trees. More than 160 years ago, Henry David Thoreau prescribed the tonic of the wilderness for the discontent of men in his *Walden: Or, Life in the Woods*. Today, the practice of *shinrin-yoku* might spark a rise in similar prescriptions.

Shinrin-yoku literally translates to 'forest bathing', or taking in the atmosphere of the forest, and refers to soaking up the sights, smells and sounds of a natural setting to promote physiological and psychological health. The term was first coined in 1982 but, today, millions of Japanese walk along forty-eight 'forest therapy' trails, to get their dose of what I guess could be labelled 'outdoorphins'.

Fans of *shinrin-yoku* explain that it differs from hiking because it is about taking everything in and stimulating all our senses, and because it focuses on the therapeutic aspects.

Professor Qing Li at the Health Nippon Medical School in Tokyo has studied the effect of *shinrin-yoku* and found that the practice reduces the levels of cortisol in the blood and boosts the immune system. But forest bathing may not be good only for our physical health. Researchers from the University of Essex have explored how being active in a natural setting affects our mood. Looking at ten different UK studies involving more than 1,200 people, the researchers found that taking part in activities like country walks, sailing and gardening had a positive effect on the mood and self-esteem of the participants. Overall, evidence is building that time spent in the natural world benefits human health.

Also in the UK, researchers have created the 'mappiness project', mapping happiness across the nation and now throughout the world. It's part of a research project at the London School of Economics and its aim is to understand how people's happiness is affected by the local environment. As they say, we can all agree that green hillsides are lovely – but we want to know *how* lovely they are. What is the quantitative evidence that a nice environment makes us feel better? The project uses real-time individual experiences, and I would encourage you to sign up. A researcher will beep you once (or more) a day on your phone to ask how you're feeling, and a few basic things to control for: who you're with, where you are, what you're doing (if you're outdoors, you can also take and send a photo). The project has already collected more than 3.5 million responses contributed by 65,000 participants.

What the researchers find is that, on average, participants are significantly and substantially happier outdoors in all green or natural habitats than they are in urban environments. This study provides new evidence on links between nature and well-being, strengthening existing evidence of a positive relationship between happiness and exposure to green or natural environments in our lives.

To sum up, there is growing evidence that nature has a positive effect on our health and happiness. In addition, *shinrin-yoku* may help you get out of your head and experience the data coming through your senses. In fact, I see a lot of parallels between *shinrin-yuko* and the increasingly popular practice of mindfulness.

HAPPINESS TIP:
INTO THE WILD

Visit the same spot in nature periodically over the course of a year and really be mindful as to how the landscape is changing each time.

Find and explore a forest. Take it slowly and forget about what would make a nice Instagram picture. Instead, listen to the wind in the leaves, watch the sun bounce off the branches, take a deep breath and see what smells you can detect. Try to visit the same spot several times a year, so you can appreciate how it changes over the seasons. Say hi to the first day of spring, summer, autumn and winter. Go alone or invite people to join you.

BRAIN BRUSHING
IN BHUTAN

In some Bhutanese schools, the students and teachers start and finish their day with a silent moment of 'brain brushing', a short mindfulness exercise.

Mindfulness has its roots in Buddhism, where the belief is that the human pursuit of everlasting happiness leads to suffering. We feel pain because nothing lasts. Mindfulness is about being present. Right here, right now, in this moment, and being loving and kind to yourself. Whereas our thoughts usually revolve around the future or the past, mindfulness is all about the present moment.

Because the Bhutanese focus on Gross National Happiness instead of Gross National Product, the country is almost a laboratory testing out different approaches to improve well-being. One of these efforts is the GNH Curriculum, which targets ten non-academic 'life skills' in secondary-school students in a collaboration between the Bhutanese Ministry of Education and a team of researchers from the University of Pennsylvania. One of these non-academic life skills is mindfulness.

More than eight thousand students participated in the study, in which the researchers randomly assigned the schools taking part either to the treatment group, which received the GNH Curriculum over fifteen months, or to the control group, which received a placebo GNH Curriculum over the same period.

The researchers tested two hypotheses. First, does the GNH Curriculum raise levels of well-being? And second, does increasing well-being improve academic performance? It found that the GNH Curriculum significantly increased student well-being and improved academic performance.

LET'S TALK ABOUT
MENTAL HEALTH

Despite the link between mental and physical health, the importance of mental health is still being overlooked and, unfortunately, mental illness is still often seen as a taboo subject.

One day, I was interviewed by a young Korean man. I was telling him that one of the reasons why I established the Happiness Research Institute was that a good friend of mine died suddenly at the age of forty-nine and, as my own mother had died at the same age, it was a wake-up call. If you are only going to live until you are forty-nine, what are you going to spend those years doing? I thought to myself. Stay in my then job, which I was not really excited about – or start something which may be risky but may also be really awesome?

At this point, the young man shared with me that his mother had also died when she was forty-nine. She had died from depression. South Korea has the highest suicide rate in the OECD, and a high incidence of depression. Depression is a disease, but it is treatable. Sadly, there is a lot of social stigma around mental illness in Korea – as in many other countries – which results in a lack of treatment, sometimes with disastrous consequences.

Out of the twenty-eight OECD countries, South Korea ranks twenty-seventh when it comes to the consumption of antidepressants; Denmark ranks seventh. Does this mean that Danes are more depressed than the Koreans? No, it just means they are getting some sort of treatment. Whether medication is the right sort of treatment is up for discussion, but it is a good thing to be a society in which treatment for mental illness is available and affordable (subsidized by the government) and in which the stigma around mental illness has been reduced sufficiently that people feel able to seek treatment.

To fight the stigma that surrounds mental illness, we need to listen more and learn more. We need to end the misunderstanding and the prejudice. We need to end whispering about mental illnesses behind closed doors. We need to say the scary words out loud, so they lose their power, and so no one has to struggle on in silence.

We should salute those who are working against the idea that mental illness is something that should be covered up. A couple of years ago, a number of Danish writers, models and movie directors participated in a series on national television about the mental illnesses they had been dealing with. More recently, Prince Harry has been open about the challenges he has faced. He said he had been 'very close to a complete breakdown on numerous occasions' and is now encouraging more people to reach out to others in times of need and to normalize conversation about mental health. 'The experience I have had is that, once you start talking about it, you realize that actually you're part of quite a big club,' he said to the *Telegraph* in April 2017.

It is because of actions like this that the UK and Denmark rank first and third when it comes to reducing stigma and increasing awareness, according to the Economist Intelligence Unit's Mental Integration Index. It is time for every society to become much more open about mental illness, just as it is about other illnesses. So, let me just add my two cents and tell you that my mother also suffered from depression. There is no reason not to be open about that. The silver lining for South Korea here is that the young man who lost his mother to depression is now heading the Stella Foundation, which aims to create awareness and openness about depression in South Korea. He gave me a frame that holds three Korean masks, as a symbol of the fight against the masks we hide behind. The frame now stands next to my desk in my office at home.

HAPPINESS TIP:
START TALKING ABOUT MENTAL HEALTH

Next time you ask someone how they are doing, have a real interest in their answer, and do not accept 'fine'.

According to the Mental Health Foundation in the UK, nearly half of adults in the country believe that, in their lifetime, they have had a diagnosable mental health problem, yet only a third have received a diagnosis; and every week, one in six adults experiences symptoms of a common mental health problem, such as anxiety or depression. Don't be afraid to ask friends, family members or colleagues the question 'But how are you *really* doing?' And don't accept a one-word answer. On mentalhealth.gov (you'll find it under the US Department of Health and Human Services), there is a lot of advice if you need to start a conversation with a friend or family member about mental health. It suggests ways to bring the subject up, such as 'I've been worried about you. Can we talk about what you are experiencing? If not, who are you comfortable talking to? It seems like you are going through a difficult time. How can I help you to find help?' Or 'I am someone who cares and wants to listen. What do you want me to know about how you are feeling?'

HEALTH

Commuting as exercise

Copenhagen: In Copenhagen, 45 per cent of all commutes for work or education are by bike. This is part of the reason why Danes get more exercise than most people, and without hitting the gym. Read more on pp. 131–4.

Ciclovía

Bogotá, Columbia: Every Sunday, more than a hundred kilometres of streets are closed to motor vehicles and converted to walkable, bikeable and playable areas. More than a million make use of this opportunity. Read more on pp. 140–41.

Shinrin-yoku

Japan: 'Forest bathing' refers to soaking up the sights, smells and sounds of a natural setting to promote physiological and psychological health. Read more on pp. 149–51.

Brain brushing

Bhutan: Students and teachers start and finish their day with a silent moment doing a short mindfulness exercise to improve their well-being and academic performance. Read more on pp. 152–3.

Reducing the stigma of mental illness

UK: The UK gets top ranking in reducing the stigma associated with and increasing awareness of mental illness, according to the Economist Intelligence Unit's Mental Integration Index. There is still a long way to go in all countries, but the recent campaign launched by the royal family to recruit celebrities and other individuals to make videos discussing depression or anxiety is a step in the right direction. Read more on pp. 154–6.

The scenic route

US: Researchers from Yahoo! Labs have developed an algorithm that calculates the most pleasant and enjoyable route from your location to your destination. As an example, the fastest route from the home of Paul Revere to the state capital in Boston will take you through car-lined streets. Adding just two minutes of travel time, you can instead walk through quieter areas and enjoy famous city landmarks.

Sports candy

Reykjavik, Iceland: The TV show *Lazy Town* uses an athletic protagonist who lives on a diet consisting of fruits and vegetables to encourage the children to take part in physical activities outdoors and to eat healthily. The hero is contrasted with the show's lazy, junk-food-eating villain and antagonist. In cooperation with a major supermarket chain in Iceland, fruit and vegetables were branded as 'sports candy' (as in the TV show), and this resulted in a 22 per cent increase in sales of fruit and vegetables.

CHAPTER SIX

—

FREEDOM

FREEDOM

Let me ask you one question: 'Are you satisfied or dissatisfied with your freedom to choose what you do with your life?' What is certain is that having the freedom to choose what we do with our lives – feeling that we are the captain of our destiny – is linked to happiness.

'No people can be truly happy if they do not feel that they are choosing the course of their own life,' states the World Happiness Report 2012 – and it also finds that having this freedom of choice is one of the six factors that explain why some people are happier than others.

In Denmark, there is freedom of expression, freedom of assembly and the freedom to marry whomever you like – as long as that other person says yes, of course. Otherwise, me and Rachel Weisz would be a thing.

According to the Human Freedom Index 2015, an annual report that presents the state of human freedom in the world, Denmark ranks fourth, after Hong Kong, Switzerland and Finland. The UK comes in at 9th place, the US 20th, Russia 111th, China 132nd, Saudi Arabia 141st and, last, at 152nd, is Iran.

'No people can be truly happy
if they do not feel that they are
choosing the course of their own life'

World Happiness Report 2012

The index looks at classical rights like freedom of movement, assembly, expression, and so on, but has more than seventy indicators, including autonomy of religious organizations, freedom of media content, the treatment of same-sex relationships, divorce and equal inheritance rights.

However, I think there is one key factor when it comes to freedom that the Human Freedom Index overlooks: time, a resource that is shared out equally among us all. Every day, we each get 1,440 minutes and, every week, we each get 168 hours. However, we have very different levels of freedom when it comes to how we spend our time. In this chapter, we will look at three areas that impact on your freedom or how you spend your time – at work, with your family and on your commute – and see if there are lessons we can learn from the happiest people.

LAND OF THE FREE

'When it comes to increasing our quality of life, I think moving to Copenhagen is the best decision that we have made as a family.'

Kate and her husband, Simon, moved from London five years ago with their first child, when Simon was offered a job in Denmark. Since then, the family has grown to four. It was a leap of faith: Kate has since found a communications job in Copenhagen but gave up a well-paid job in London, at first to concentrate on bringing up their child, and neither Simon nor Kate had been to Denmark before.

'We were just tired: tired of the long working hours; tired of the long commute; tired of feeling a bit like strangers when we finally had time at the weekends. I go to bed early and Simon worked really long hours, so some days we wouldn't see each other at all.'

If there is one thing all expats in Denmark mention, it is the work–life balance. 'You have a fundamentally different approach to time here. You value that families have time to eat together, every day. We might have earned more in London, but we had far less time.'

For many expats, the greatest change is in fact the shift in work–life balance; they describe Danish offices as being like morgues after 5 p.m. If you work at the weekend, Danes suspect you are a madman working on some secret project.

'I think the main difference between the British and the Danish work culture is the unabashed value placed on free time. You value time with family and friends. You leave work at 4 p.m. or 5 p.m. And no excuse is needed. Last week, I left the office at five, I cycled home – I have gone full-on Danish – and was home twenty minutes later. Simon had picked up the girls and was preparing dinner.'

The notion in Scandinavia seems to be that it takes two people to make a baby, so it should be the equal responsibility of those two people to raise that child. 'At work, the men will say they can't make a meeting at 4 p.m. because they have to pick up their kids. That would never happen in London.'

And the data echoes Kate's experience. According to the OECD, Danes enjoy one of the best balances between work and play in the world. The average annual hours worked per worker is 1,457 in Denmark, compared to 1,674 in the UK, 1,790 in the US and an OECD average of 1,766. Danes also enjoy a high level of flexibility at work – working from home and choosing what time to start their working day. Meeting deadlines and showing up punctually at meetings is more important than when or where you carry out your work. In addition, there is a minimum of five weeks' paid holiday for all employees.

Work–life Balance

1. Netherlands	13. Hungary	26. United Kingdom
2. Denmark	14. Estonia	27. Chile
3. France	15. Italy	28. New Zealand
4. Spain	16. Czech Republic	29. Brazil
5. Belgium	17. Switzerland	30. United States
6. Norway	18. Slovak Republic	31. Australia
7. Sweden	19. Slovenia	32. South Africa
8. Germany	20. Greece	33. Iceland
9. Russian Federation	21. Canada	34. Japan
	22. Austria	35. Israel
10. Ireland	23. Portugal	36. Korea
11. Luxembourg	24. Poland	37. Mexico
12. Finland	25. Latvia	38. Turkey

Source: OECD Better Life Index

Fifty-two weeks of paid leave per child are allocated by the state, and these can be divided between you and your partner. The amount you receive depends on a range of factors, including your salary, and whether you work full time. However, even if you are unemployed, you will receive around 18,000 kroner (around £2,000) per month from the state. Child care is subsidized, too, which brings the price tag for parents to about £300 per month per child.

The differences in work–life balance, the family-friendly policies and the level of freedom parents experience are clear when we look at the happiness 'price' of being a parent: the so-called 'parental happiness gap'.

THE PARENTAL
HAPPINESS GAP

—————

*There is no doubt that kids are great sources of joy
and love; at the same time, they are sources of stress,
frustration and worry.*

Loving your children and believing they are the greatest thing in the
world is not the same as having a stress-free experience. Children
provide parents with purpose and demand a sacrifice of parental
freedom in return. So how do kids affect our happiness? Is there
any truth in the statement that parents are only as happy as their
unhappiest child?

Usually, happiness studies find that parents are less happy than
their oh-I-really-don't-know-what-I-will-spend-all-my-weekend-
doing-besides-going-to-Starbucks-binge-watching-*Westworld*-going-
for-drinks-working-on-my-novel-relaxing-and-maybe-going-to-the-
gym non-parent peers.

This is known as the parental happiness gap, or the parental
happiness penalty, and it has prompted headlines like 'HOW
HAVING CHILDREN ROBS PARENTS OF THEIR HAPPINESS'
and 'YOU ARE LESS HAPPY WHEN YOU HAVE A CHILD,
STUDY SAYS'. However, I think that some of the nuances are often
lost when such stories make the news.

First of all, while children may have a negative impact on one dimension of happiness (such as overall life satisfaction), having them is found to have a positive effect on another dimension of happiness – the eudemonic dimension, which focuses on the sense of purpose or meaning in life.

Second, children have a different impact on the happiness of women and that of men, as women, traditionally, have taken on a greater share of the responsibility and burden of raising kids. According to Luca Stanca, professor and author of 'The Geography of Parenthood and Well-being', the parenting penalty is 65 per cent higher for women.

Third, kids come in different sizes and ages. While a one-year-old baby who denies you your sleep for months may make you miserable right now, fifty years from now that child may be a source of joy when you're sitting in a retirement home. Studies also show that, among widows and widowers, having a child has a positive effect on life satisfaction. Something to bear in mind with all these stories is that 'Having Kids Makes People Less Happy' is better clickbait than 'Studies Show the Effects of Children on Happiness are Mixed, depending on the Dimensions of Happiness Measured and the Complexity of a Dynamic Lifetime Relationship'.

Life satisfaction premium

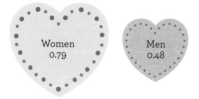

Women
0.79

Men
0.48

Source: Luca Stanca, 'The Geography of Parenthood and Well-being: Do Children Make Us Happy? Where and Why?' in the World Happiness Report – Special Rome Edition, 2016.

But that still leaves us with the question of why parents with young kids report lower levels of overall life satisfaction than their non-parent peers. Well, what we see is that the happiness gap depends on *where* we measure it. Parents in the US are 12 per cent less satisfied with their life than their non-parent peers; in Britain, the gap is 8 per cent; in Denmark, it is 3 per cent. There is a small happiness gap in Sweden and Norway of around 2 per cent – but in Sweden and Norway parents are happier than people without kids. The Scandinavian countries consistently come out on top in family-friendly rankings; however, Sweden outperforms Denmark for balancing family and work. For instance, Swedish parents are entitled to spend sixty days a year at home caring for a sick child under the age of twelve.

A team of researchers led by Jennifer Glass, a professor of sociology at the University of Texas, examined the parental happiness gap and the level of freedom parents could enjoy in each country. Among the questions they asked were: Is childcare affordable? Is leave available to look after a sick child? Is paid holiday given? In other words, are parents provided with the tools and freedom which help them to combine working and having a family? The results showed that the happiness gap was explained by differences in such family-friendly policies. In countries with the best packages, the parental happiness penalty was eliminated. However, the happiest parents seem to be found in Portugal.

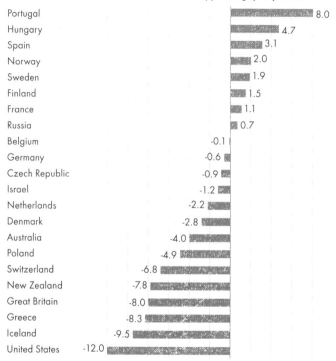

Parental happiness gap in per cent

Portugal	8.0
Hungary	4.7
Spain	3.1
Norway	2.0
Sweden	1.9
Finland	1.5
France	1.1
Russia	0.7
Belgium	-0.1
Germany	-0.6
Czech Republic	-0.9
Israel	-1.2
Netherlands	-2.2
Denmark	-2.8
Australia	-4.0
Poland	-4.9
Switzerland	-6.8
New Zealand	-7.8
Great Britain	-8.0
Greece	-8.3
Iceland	-9.5
United States	-12.0

Source: Glass, Simon and Anderson: 'Parenthood and Happiness:
Effects of Work–Family Reconciliation Policies in 22 OECD
Countries', 2016.

In Portugal, grandparents serve as a fundamental support base for parents and have a functional role in the raising of grandchildren. According to a comprehensive study which was initiated in 2005 and has since monitored the routines of six thousand children and thousands of parents and grandparents, Portuguese grandparents play a key role in the day-to-day life of Portuguese families and help with the daily routine of looking after their grandchildren. An impressive 72 per cent said that grandparents were their primary partners in the education of their children and helped with homework and extracurricular activities. When six grown-ups instead of two take an active part in and responsibility for accompanying the kids to school, supervising homework, cooking, taking the kids to sports and other clubs and doing other chores, it provides the parents with more freedom and free time – and, as it turns out, greater levels of happiness.

Jennifer Glass explained to the *New York Times* that all the countries surveyed had more extensive policies to support working families than the US. This issue has also been raised by British comedian and host of the TV show *Last Week Tonight* John Oliver, who pointed out in a Mother's Day special that US and Papua New Guinea are the only two countries in the world that do not have a policy in place to give mothers paid time off after having a baby, and added that, if America really loved its mothers, then it would go beyond celebrating them once a year and implement a policy that would help them in their daily lives.

Until the US addresses this issue, according to Oliver, the only message that should go out on Mother's Day is: 'Mothers – we owe everything to them. They gave birth to us, they nurtured us, and they made us who we are. And this Mother's Day, we have just one thing to say to all the mothers out there: Get the fuck back to work.'

HAPPINESS TIP:
CREATE BONUS GRANDPARENTS

We all benefit from relationships across generational divides. Consider who might make good bonus grandparents or just a senior buddy for you.

In a perfect world, we would all have Scandinavian family policies and Portuguese grandparents. Our parents may no longer be alive, or they may not live close enough to give their support in helping with the kids. To try to fill this gap, several cities in Denmark have now created 'Bonus Grandparents Systems' where senior citizens volunteer to be a foster grandparent for a specific family. For instance, the bonus nanny will help if the kids are sick but will also take part in family celebrations and activities. Although the system has already been set up in Denmark, you could create something similar yourself. An extra pair of hands, a different experience for the children and an extra source of patience to draw on can be helpful. And another upside is that it also reduces loneliness in older generations. Meeting your neighbours through the mini-library or the community garden you set up may be a good first step to build the necessary relationship and trust.

CASE STUDY
LOUISE & TOM

'One of the great privileges of the author's life is that you can make the world your home. When I sprang from my comfortable university career into a new life in a foreign country, I took a big risk.'

'Some of the best decisions we make come from that inner voice that says, "Why not?" That says, "*Andiamo*." So much disappointment arises from what is desired but not chosen.' So wrote Frances Mayes, author of *Under the Tuscan Sun*, in the *Guardian* in 2016. She turned her personal story into a book, which turned into a bestseller, which turned into a movie, which turned millions of people across the world into dreamers. Two of those dreamers were Louise and her husband, Tom.

A couple of years ago, they moved from the US to Italy. 'We both looked for jobs overseas, and Tom was lucky enough to land one.'

Louise now works as a freelance journalist, and we spoke on the phone. When I learned their story, I had as many questions for her as she did for me. When she spoke to me about their new life in Italy, I could tell she was smiling.

They now live in Florence, the capital of Tuscany, by the Arno River, a city that is home to around four hundred thousand people. It's quite the contrast to New York. The pace of life, the sounds, the smells, the colours – all are completely different. Buy tomatoes at the San Lorenzo market and you will see shades of red you never knew existed.

Louise and Tom brought their five-month-old daughter with them when they moved, and they soon discovered that the attitude to how you raise children is different in Italy, too. Their daughter's feet are tickled by strangers, and they will also tell the parents that 8 p.m. is way too early to put a toddler to bed. But it was also having their daughter that made them look for positions overseas.

'We left the US to go to Italy mainly because of the insane childcare prices back home. Here, we can get it at a fraction of the price – and we are in Italy . . .'

Not everything is like a Hollywood movie, though. 'We miss our friends and family back home, of course, but we are happy we came. We have more time to be a family here.'

THINK OUTSIDE
THE BOSS: HAPPY
ENTREPRENEURS

On the Statue of Liberty, a plaque famously reads:

> *Give me your tired, your poor, your*
> *huddled masses yearning to breathe free.*

Speaking to Louise made me understand that the tired are increasingly seeking somewhere else to breathe free. However, leaving the country you live in may be a little too drastic for most. For some, changing boss might be an easier switch.

Around five years ago, I told my dad that I was quitting my job. I had a well-paid secure job as international director for a think tank which focused on sustainability.

'So, what are you going to do instead?' he asked.

'Well, I am going to study happiness. I want to build a think tank called the Happiness Research Institute.'

There was silence for a second.

'I think that sounds like a great idea.'

Some might have thought that starting a think tank on happiness was not the best career move in the wake of a global recession, but I remember my dad telling me at a very early age that you should not focus on potential earnings when it comes to a job but on the satisfaction you would get from doing it. 'You are going to spend a huge part of your life working – it should be something you enjoy.'

> *'One should not focus on potential earnings when it comes to jobs – one should focus on the satisfaction you would get from it.'*
>
> **Wolf Wiking**

The first years were tough. No money. No free time. I had never worked so hard, earned so little – and had so much fun. And I am not the only one to have had that experience.

'I don't even think we should call it work. We should call it "creating". We get to create something. And what I create is part of me. It is part of my identity. That is where true happiness comes from.' As well as being a Danish social entrepreneur in the fashion industry, Veronica is a force of nature and a beacon of joy. Last summer, I met her, her husband and their daughter after the three of them had spent a month in Peru looking for the perfect alpaca wool. When I spoke with her a year later, the family had just returned from a month in Thailand looking for the perfect silk. This time, Veronica was five months pregnant, but one thing that was common to both trips is that the family went to a prison. A women's prison.

'Well, actually, my daughter could only come to the prison with us in Peru, not Thailand,' Veronica laughs.

Veronica, after discovering that most women in prison in developing countries are incarcerated for poverty-related crimes, established the Copenhagen-based fashion label Carcel – which enables women in prison to turn wasted time into skills and paid jobs so they can support themselves, send their children to school and save up for a new, crime-free beginning, in the hope, ultimately, of breaking the cycle of poverty and crime. Each product carries the name of the woman who made it and is manufactured inside women's prisons which pay fair wages to the women to help them support themselves and their children.

Creating a business from scratch is hard work. 'I am poor, but I am happy. And yes, I work far more than I would in a normal job. But I would not trade this for any other job in the world. The biggest change is that you are your job. I am not a mother, then a director, then a girlfriend, then a friend. I am Veronica. All the time. That is what makes me so happy.'

And Veronica is not alone. According to the World Happiness Report, the self-employed are worse off in many ways, including income, hours of work and job security, but even so, they often report higher levels of overall job satisfaction than do the employed, at least in OECD countries.

Why are entrepreneurs in OECD countries happier than employees, but not in all poorer countries? The answer lies in the reason behind the decision to become an entrepreneur. Did we start our own business because we wanted to – or did we start a business because there were no opportunities in the regular labour market?

So, yes, the self-employed often work more hours than the employed. And yes, perhaps we also need to sleep on friends' couches more often because money is tight. But we are also happier. At least, that is what the studies show. The self-employed report not just higher levels of job satisfaction but also higher levels of life satisfaction.

Another reason is that the self-employed are a weird bunch. We are more optimistic than others. One of us started a business that sells Serenity Dog Pods. However, it is also clear that when people go from regular employment to self-employment, they report higher levels of life satisfaction. Why?

Entrepreneurs have a greater sense of purpose, of direction in life, but studies also confirm the widely held notion that greater freedom and the opportunity to be your own boss are sources of happiness both at work and outside work.

Entrepreneurs hardly ever have enough free time, but they do experience plenty of freedom: the freedom to pursue a passion; the freedom to say no to a client; the freedom to schedule work around the needs of the family.

'I decide where I am when. Having small kids makes it difficult to focus on your career – but being an entrepreneur allows you to design your daily life differently. Around what my kid needs first,' explains Veronica. 'If I sense my daughter is sad one morning, I will just arrive for work an hour later and I will read another book to her. I don't have a boss who tells me I can't be with my daughter now. Also, she is with us on this adventure. This will be part of her story, too. We are creating our common story together.'

However, while many desire the freedom that entrepreneurs enjoy, fewer want the risk that comes with it. So, it is worth looking for ways to enjoy greater autonomy and freedom at work as a regular employee.

FIVE WAYS TO FREE UP YOUR TIME

COOK MORE THAN YOU NEED:

Cook a bigger portion of a meal at the weekend than you will eat at one sitting, and freeze the leftovers to provide meals on other days.

USE SLACK TIME:

Make use of the time you spend waiting throughout the day – two minutes here; five minutes there. Set yourself up to make use of these time 'leftovers'. Decide beforehand what you want to spend this time doing. I spend mine on Duolingo to improve my Spanish – and since you now have started flirting with the idea of moving to Italy, why not learn a few Italian words? *Va bene?*

TWO IN ONE:

Instead of choosing between, for example, socializing and exercising, you may be able to combine them. Go for a run with your buddy, play Frisbee, go mountain biking in the woods.

TIE YOURSELF TO THE MAST:

In *The Odyssey*, Odysseus asks to be tied to the mast, in order not to give in to the temptation of the Sirens. Today, we need to find something that helps us to steer clear of time stealers like Facebook. Most people wish they spent less time browsing the internet or looking at Facebook, and apps like Freedom help you to do this, preventing you from using the internet for up to eight hours.

APPLY PARKINSON'S LAW:

You are likely to be more efficient if you have less time. If your spouse's parents call and say they are dropping by in fifteen minutes, no doubt you manage to clean the house super-efficiently. According to Cyril Northcote Parkinson, British historian and author, 'Work expands to fill the time available for its completion.' To come at this from a different angle, schedule when you have to start a task – and when you have to finish it.

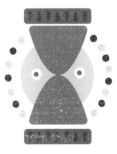

MAILS, MEETINGS
AND MANAGERS

Imagine having a full day when you are by yourself at work. There are no meetings. You won't find yourself in a conference room with eight colleagues listening to only two of those people discussing what the right solution is to some issue or other.

Your boss is not going to call you and ask for a progress report on the IT project, and no emails are ticking in with 'URGENT' in the subject line. It is a nice dream, isn't it? Imagine what you could do with that level of freedom. Imagine how much work you would get done that day. Profound work, work that needs your full attention and concentration. Work which you have chosen to do and enjoy doing.

Broadly speaking, there are three things that take away our freedom at work: meetings, managers and mails. A lot of us try to fill in the ten- or twenty-minute holes between meetings with work that requires concentration and long uninterrupted periods of time to be done properly. According to Jason Fried, serial entrepreneur and author of *Remote: Office Not Required*, meetings and managers undermine our productivity. In short, meetings are employees talking about work that they *have* done or work that they are *going* to do, and managers are people whose job it is to interrupt people. Both are killing our productivity.

As a solution, Fried suggests that, instead of casual Fridays, 'no-talk Thursdays' should be introduced. Pick a Thursday – say, the first or last of every month – and make it the rule that nobody in the office can talk to each other that day. No interruptions. No phone calls. No meetings. Just silence. Now work on whatever you need to work on.

We tried it at the Happiness Research Institute. For us, it didn't work to have a full day, or even an afternoon, when we couldn't talk to each other, so we modified it and introduced daily 'creative zones'. Two hours of uninterrupted time to get stuff that needed full concentration done.

Later, I discovered that Intel had experimented with a similar 'do-not-disturb sign on the door' model: Tuesday-morning quiet time. On two US sites, three hundred engineers and managers agreed to minimize interruptions on Tuesday mornings. No meetings were scheduled, phone calls went to voicemail, emails and IM were shut down. The aim was to ensure four hours of 'thinking time' – and to measure the effect this had. The pilot lasted seven months, 71 per cent of the participants recommended extending it to other departments and Intel found that the trial had been 'successful in improving employee effectiveness, efficiency and quality of life for numerous employees in diverse job roles'. Like Intel, I found having uninterrupted time useful and productive but, like the Happiness Research Institute, your workplace might need a different modification again.

For some people, no-talk Thursdays or quiet Tuesday mornings are similar in concept to working from home. No meetings, no interruptions. In Denmark, there is a high level of autonomy and flexibility in the workplace and people are often allowed to carry out a proportion of their work at home. This is part of the reason why 94 per cent of Danes say they are happy with their working conditions, at least according to the Eurobarometer, which has been measuring public opinion on behalf of the European Commission since 1973.

However, I think a bigger reason for this happiness is that 58 per cent of Danes (according to YouGov) say they would continue to work even if they no longer had to for financial reasons – say, if they won 10 million kroner in the lottery. Work can – and should – be a source of happiness; and the proper design and functioning of the workplace can push more of us closer to this. And one part of this proper design is to provide people with an element of freedom: free time without interruptions. This may also entail not showing up at the office.

HAPPINESS TIP:
DO-NOT-DISTURB INITIATIVES

Try out initiatives like Tuesday-morning quiet time which may improve your sense of freedom at work.

Start a conversation at work about the ways in which flexibility and autonomy might improve employee satisfaction and productivity. Could you or your boss introduce concepts like quiet Tuesday mornings – carve out two or three hours every Tuesday morning in which no meetings are scheduled, no phone calls made or emails sent? Convince them to have a trial period of a month or two, and then evaluate it in terms of employee satisfaction and productivity. Or you could suggest work-from-home Wednesdays. If an employee saves two hours driving to work, they might even put in an extra hour for the company – and still gain an hour of free time.

MIND THE GAP

I propose a new mandatory course for all university students. Every student in the class is squeezed into the smallest wardrobe possible and they have to stand there for forty-five minutes without making eye contact with anyone.

If you make eye contact, you fail. Then they are asked to move into an even smaller wardrobe – in which they won't all fit. If you don't make it into the second wardrobe, you fail the course. I call it 'Commuting 101'.

I'm not sure how long Jean-Paul Sartre's commute was, but it might have been where he first came up with the phrase 'Hell is other people.' Granted, some commuters do get some pleasure and value out of their commute: they read, listen to music or simply digest the day. However, for many, the daily commute is a drag, and we find it frustrating because it makes us feel like we don't have any control. You are trapped on the bus, or in the train, or in the car.

The idea that the car is the ultimate symbol of freedom is quintessentially American, but car advertisements the world over promise that you will be driving on meandering roads by the coast, surrounded by nature, with no other car in sight. In reality, we are more likely to be surrounded by traffic congestion and inching our way through rush hour while horns play a symphony of anger and frustration. That feels a long way from freedom. The car has become a ball and chain – it seems only to take us further away from happiness.

To make matters worse, for many, commuting to work is the worst part of the day. At least, that is what is suggested by some studies, in which people have been asked to rate different activities. Daniel Kahneman, a Nobel Prize-winning psychologist, conducted a study using the Daily Report Method, whereby respondents detail everything they did the day before – what they did and at what time, who they were with, and how they felt during each activity. In it, 909 American women rated their morning commute as the worst time of the day. Then came work – and then came the commute home.

Unfortunately, we spend a substantial part of our lives commuting. There is a lot of variation, obviously. According to a study by the OECD, people in South Africa and South Korea spend roughly twice as much time commuting per day as people in Ireland and Denmark. However, the longest commute is said to be in Bangkok, where people spend an average of two hours each day on their way to and from work.

There is also a lot of variation within countries. In the UK, people working in London endure the longest average commute (seventy-four minutes), and it has also been reported that almost 2 million Britons are travelling three hours or more for work daily.

Commuting Time

Source: OECD, 'How's Life? Measuring Well-being: Commuting Time', 2011

In a time when more and more of us are finding it difficult to juggle work and life and fit it all into the twenty-four hours of a day, it may not come as a surprise that, according to the Office of National Statistics, happiness seems to decrease with every mile a commuter travels.

Using people who travel between one and fifteen minutes to get to work as the benchmark or reference group, it becomes clear that everyone else – those who need longer than that to get to work – feels less happy, while people who work from home (or live very close to their workplace) are happier.

We see the same pattern if we examine the question of anxiety. People working from home are less anxious than others. However, it is interesting to notice that people travelling more than three hours for work are no more anxious than people who have a one-to fifteen-minute commute. We do not fully understand why the negative effects of the commute seem to vanish once you hit three hours. Perhaps this group can make better use of their commute by reading or working – and perhaps they have made a conscious choice to work in London but live in the countryside and the benefits of their living environment counteract the negative effect of the commute.

Looking across several indicators of well-being, the worst effects of commuting are associated with journeys lasting between an hour and an hour and a half.

Jessica had one of those commutes. After getting a job in advertising in San Francisco, she found herself driving 90 kilometres each way. If she hit rush hour, the commute could eat up to four hours each day. But the money was good and the extra cash could help fund expensive fertility treatments.

However, the long commute, after a long work day, took its toll on the thirty-five-year-old. She developed stress-related stomach problems, became depressed and developed pinched nerves in her lower back from so much time sitting behind the wheel.

Nine months later, she had left her job and become self-employed, working as a freelance designer and photographer. The pay was less – but she could work from home. When the BBC reported on her story in July 2016 she was six months pregnant.

FREEDOM

Work–life balance

Denmark: Danes enjoy one of the best balances between work and play in the world. A standard working week is thirty-seven hours. Danes also enjoy a high level of flexibility at work, for example working from home and choosing at what time they start their working day. Read more on pp. 166–7.

Universal basic income

Finland: In 2017, a two-year social experiment was launched in which two thousand citizens were given a guaranteed income of 560 euros a month, regardless of income, wealth or employment status. The Finns hope it will cut red tape, reduce poverty and boost employment.

Thirty-hour working week

Sweden: Several public employers and private companies are experimenting with shorter working days and weeks. One of them is the SEO (search engine optimization) company Brath, which reports: 'Today we get more done in six hours than comparable companies do in eight. We believe it brings with it the high level of creativity demanded in this line of work. We believe nobody can be creative and productive for eight hours straight. Six hours is more reasonable, even though we, too, of course, check Facebook or the news at times.'

There is no place like roam

Budapest, Hungary: Now that work does not always have to be done in the office, and with improved digital connectivity, more and more freelancers and entrepreneurs are thinking out of the cubicle and working from abroad. Budapest, Bangkok and Berlin come out on top on the list of destinations for digital nomads. One month's rent for a one-bedroom apartment in the centre of the Hungarian capital is around $500 – and a cup of coffee in a café will set you back only $1.25.

Live Near Your Work Program

Maryland, USA: The program gives monetary rewards of up to $3,000 towards the purchase, down-payments on or final costs of new homes for people who move within eight kilometres of their workplace. Participants consequently spend less time commuting and a substantial number have switched their mode of transport from driving to walking.

No emails after work

Germany: In 2011, Volkswagen stopped its BlackBerry servers sending emails to a proportion of its employees when they are off-shift. The staff can still use their devices to make calls, but the servers stop routing emails thirty minutes after the end of employees' shifts, and start again thirty minutes before they return to work. (This did not apply to senior management.)

CHAPTER SEVEN

———

TRUST

TRUST SPOTTING

One evening in 1997, Anette went to a restaurant in New York. The restaurant had a seating area outside which was marked off with a chain, and Anette let her daughter sleep there in her pram, watching her through the window.

However, Anette was soon arrested and handcuffed, and only narrowly escaped jail for child neglect. To offer up a defence: she did what most parents in Denmark do.

Travel to Copenhagen and, once you have got used to the number of bikes on the roads, you will notice something else: children sleeping outside in strollers in public spaces. While their mums and dads enjoy a cup of coffee indoors, little Gustav and little Freja are tucked up outside the cafés. Go to the countryside, and you can find vegetable stands by the road, unmanned. You grab what you want and put the cash in the box.

Trust is not only something you see, it is something that is shown to you. One afternoon, I went to pick my bike up from the repair man – but, distrait as I am, I had left my wallet at home. 'No worries. Take your bike and bring me the money tomorrow,' the repair man said. The same day, I had to read and sign a six-page contract to write a one-page editorial for an American media outlet. The bike repair man made my day better (and built my loyalty towards using him again); contracts for simple transactions make only lawyers' days better.

In an article 'Happy in Denmark – How Come?' in *Forbes Magazine*, Erika Andersen describes having had a similar experience when she visited Denmark in order to find out why the country always does so well in the happiness rankings. During her visit, she went horse-riding and wanted to hire a horse. The stable did not accept credit cards, but the owner said that Erika could go riding now and come back later with the cash.

After this, Erika came to the straightforward conclusion that Danes are happy because of the high level of trust in their society. And Erika is on to something, because trust is one of the six factors that explain why some countries are happier than others. According to the World Happiness Report 2015, 'A successful society is one in which people have a high level of trust in each other – including family members, colleagues, friends, strangers and institutions such as government. Social trust spurs a sense of life satisfaction.'

People who trust other people are happier, and trust *does* make life easier. High levels of trust exist in offices across Denmark. You don't need to write up a contract for every small transaction. A deal is a deal. Your word is your word. In Denmark, your managers will not micromanage you but simply trust that the work will be done within the agreed timelines, unless informed otherwise – and of course you are working when you are working from home.

You call the CEO by their first name, just as you do everybody else, and you have lunch at the same table and talk openly about both your work and your private life. You base your success on collaboration and teamwork rather than striving to be the star.

This spirit of cooperation, equality and trust in workplaces in Denmark is no coincidence. As we will see, social skills, cooperation, empathy and trust are part of the curriculum in Danish schools and something all Danes are encouraged to carry on into our adult lives.

Percentage of people expressing a high level of trust in others

Denmark: **89%**

Norway: **88%**

Finland: **86%**

Sweden: **84%**

Netherlands: **80%**

Switzerland: **74%**

Estonia: **72%**

Israel: **71%**

New Zealand: **69%**

United Kingdom: **69%**

Belgium: **69%**

Australia: **64%**

Spain: **62%**

Austria: **62%**

Germany: **61%**

Japan: **61%**

OECD average: **59%**

France: **56%**

Ireland: **56%**

Czech Republic: **56%**

Slovenia: **53%**

United States: **49%**

Poland: **47%**

Slovak Republic: **47%**

Hungary: **47%**

Korea: **46%**

Greece: **40%**

Portugal: **38%**

Mexico: **26%**

Turkey: **24%**

Chile: **13%**

Source: OECD: 'Society at a Glance – Social Indicators', 2011

HAPPINESS TIP:

ENCOURAGE PRAISE AMONG CO-WORKERS TO INCREASE TRUST

Employee of the week is the one who has made their colleagues shine or told other people about their achievements.

Employee of the week is far from a new invention, but this model is a little different, because the flowers are not given to the employee who has done the best job but to the colleague who has praised others. If Jørgen has done a great job and Sigrid has told the boss about how well he's done, Sigrid will receive the flowers.

A few years ago, this model was used at the intensive neurological ward at Copenhagen's largest hospital, which had been having challenges with a large amount of sick days being taken. The climate was characterized by mistrust, job satisfaction was low and staff turnover was high. So, the department started to give a bouquet of flowers to the employee of the week, as part of a larger focus on using praise to create motivation. The strategy resulted in sick days being reduced by almost 75 per cent.

THE LOST WALLET
EXPERIMENT

> *'In general, do you think most people can be trusted, or, alternatively, that you can't be too careful when you're dealing with people?'*

This is a standard question to measure trust and has been used in many surveys, over many years, in many countries. What would you answer? Do you trust people? Would you trust them to return your wallet if they found it on the street, with cash in it? Sometimes, when it comes to trust, we don't give people the credit they deserve.

The Canadian General Social Survey found that people in Toronto believe that the chance of their wallet being returned with the money still in it if found by a stranger is less than 25 per cent. However, when twenty wallets were 'dropped' in different locations of Toronto to study the actual number, it turned out that 80 per cent were returned.

The lost wallet experiment – a measure of trustworthiness – was first conducted by *Reader's Digest Europe* in 1996. Wallets, each containing cash, a name and an address, were left on streets in twenty cities in fourteen European countries and in a dozen cities in the US. In two countries, all the wallets were returned with the money still inside: Norway and Denmark.

In 2013, *Reader's Digest* repeated the experiment. This time, researchers 'dropped' twelve wallets in sixteen cities. Each wallet contained a name, a mobile phone number, a family photo, coupons, business cards and the equivalent of $50 in local currency. How many wallets would you expect to be returned with the money still inside them?

So, if you guessed close to 50 per cent across all sixteen countries, you were right. In total, 192 wallets were dropped and 90 were returned.

Number of wallets returned (of twelve)

Helsinki,
Finland

Mumbai,
India

Budapest,
Hungary

New York,
USA

Moscow,
Russia

Amsterdam,
Netherlands

Berlin,
Germany

Ljubljana,
Slovenia

London,
England

Warsaw,
Poland

Bucharest,
Romania

Rio de Janeiro,
Brazil

Zurich,
Switzerland

Prague,
Czech Republic

Madrid,
Spain

Lisbon,
Portugal

In Rio, seventy-three-year-old Delma returned a wallet because, as a teen, she had shoplifted a magazine but was found out by her mother and told that that kind of behaviour was unacceptable. The lesson stuck with her. In London, one of the five wallets that were returned was handed in by Ursula, mid-thirties and originally from Poland. 'If you find money, you can't assume it belongs to a rich man. It might be the last bit of money a mother has to feed her family,' she said. In Ljubljana, Manca, a twenty-one-year-old student, returned the wallet with the money. 'Once, I lost an entire bag,' she told the researchers, 'but I got everything back. So I know what it feels like.'

Ursula and Manca obviously have a strong sense of empathy. They put themselves in the shoes of those who had lost the wallet. To me, there is a link between empathy, cooperation and trust. If we have strong empathetic skills, we are more inclined to cooperate than to compete and, when we all cooperate, we are more inclined to trust each other.

That is why, if we choose empathy over selfishness, we will all be better off. If this transmutes into being trustworthy, we will all be better off. If we understand the value of cooperation over competition, we will all be better off. In a society that rests on empathy, cooperation and trust, we will all be better off – and happier.

So, let's start by being reliable, by keeping our word and keeping secrets if people have confided in us. Loyalty to those not present proves our loyalty to those who are. Being trustworthy is a valuable asset, both in our own life, and to the lives of the people we care about.

Perhaps Mark Twain said it best:

> *'If you tell the truth, you don't have to remember anything.'*

This makes for an easier, more relaxed and happier life. If that weren't enough, having empathy may also make us financially better off in the long run. The study 'Early Social-emotional Functioning and Public Health: The Relationship between Kindergarten Social Competence and Future Wellness', which was published in the *American Journal of Public Health* in 2015, followed hundreds of kids from their time in kindergarten to nearly two decades on. The researchers found statistically significant associations between the social and emotional skills the kids demonstrated in kindergarten and their lives as adults in terms of education, employment, substance use, mental health and crime.

RAISING HAPPINESS

▌ *'Maths and Danish are important, but so
▌ are the children's social skills – and, yes,
▌ their happiness.'*

Louise is a teacher and, like most Danish teachers, is as concerned
with her pupils' overall well-being and social and emotional
development as she is with their academic performance.

Up until recently, the most popular class for kids was 'klassens
time' – 'the class's hour'. It is a weekly lesson in which the teacher
and the kids discuss different issues. The kids take turns to bring
cake or treats which can be shared during klassens time. The topics
discussed could include: Has there been any bullying in the past
week? What board game should we buy for the class now that we
have saved sufficient money to buy one? Is someone feeling left
out? In my opinion, one of the biggest policy mistakes that has been
made in Denmark in recent times is a school reform that changed
the class hour. From having a dedicated timeslot each week, the
class hour is now 'integrated' – policy speak for 'abolished' – into
other subjects.

But still the Danish education system prioritizes the teaching of
empathy, and the kids often work in groups – something they will
need to learn in order to manage their job in the future but which
also teaches them social skills and the value of cooperation.

'We look at the coherent development of the child – academically, socially and emotionally. Maths and science are important, but so are empathy, understanding how to be a good friend and knowing how to work with others,' Louise explains.

'The kids are shown pictures with different facial expressions on them, and we talk about the different emotions that people feel and why they may feel that way. This is also useful when we read stories. I find that good fiction enables the kids to get inside the head of the characters, to put them in the shoes of somebody else. I think good books can help; the children become more empathetic.'

Louise's view is supported by research from the New School for Social Research in New York. The results of five experiments involving more than a thousand participants showed that reading literary fiction improves our ability to detect and understand other people's emotions. But it can't just be any sort of fiction.

The researchers distinguished between 'popular fiction' (where the author leads you by the hand as a reader) and 'literary fiction' (in which you must find your own way and fill in the gaps). Instead of being told why a certain character behaves as they do, you have to figure it out yourself. That way, the book becomes not just a simulation of a social experience, it is a social experience.

There is also evidence to support the notion that teaching empathy reduces bullying. In 2015, a study asked how many boys between the ages of eleven and fifteen had felt bullied within the previous month, and 6 per cent of Danish boys reported that they had. In the UK, 50 per cent more reported having been bullied (9 per cent), and almost twice as many felt bullied in the US (11 per cent). Austria reported the most bullying (21 per cent) and the Swedish the least (4 per cent), according to the OECD report 'Skills for Social Progress: The Power of Social and Emotional Skills'.

Fortunately, Danes do not have a monopoly on teaching empathy. Recently, there was a story about a group of sixth graders learning to bridge political divides after the US election. The Millennium School, an independent and progressive school in the heart of San Francisco, and one of the most progressive institutions in the US, found students loudly voicing their disagreement in distress and disbelief on 9 November 2016 when shown footage of Trump supporters talking. But when the teachers showed the footage again, without the volume, the students noticed the fear, anger and sorrow in the supporters' faces and responded with empathy towards their fellow human beings – and this provided a different starting point for understanding why voters voted as they did.

The Danish education system is far from perfect, but I think there are several things we can take away from it. A focus on empathy and collaboration is one thing, but equally important is the understanding that success does not have to be a zero-sum game. Just because you win, it does not mean that I lose.

Education systems that rank their students are teaching them that success is a zero-sum game. If you do well, it undermines someone else's opportunities. But happiness should not be like this.

In fact, it is one thing that does not become smaller when it is shared. In Denmark, the students are not ranked. And the kids do not receive formal grades until eighth grade. Instead, there is a teacher–parent conversation about the child's development, academically, socially and emotionally, each year.

Despite the fact that the Danish education system focuses on life skills as well as maths and reading, this does not mean that Danish children do badly when it comes to academic skills. In the latest PISA (Programme for International Student Assessment) Survey (2015), which measures the academic performance of children in more than 70 countries, Danish pupils scored 511 in maths, while the scores were 492 in the UK and 470 in the US. For reading, the scores were: Denmark, 500; the UK, 498; and the US, 497.

Teaching our kids teamwork, social skills, collaboration, empathy and trustworthiness does not have to come at the expense of academic skills. Also, we may need to teach employers that trust is good for the bottom line of the company.

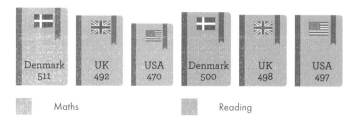

| Denmark | UK | USA | Denmark | UK | USA |
| 511 | 492 | 470 | 500 | 498 | 497 |

Maths   Reading

Source: PISA (Programme for International Student Assessment) Survey (2015)

TRUST IS CHEAP

*For people working in organizations in which there
is little trust, work is often associated with words like
'control', 'monitor', 'check up' and 'bureaucracy', with
rules and regulations.*

'We are supposed to register on our handheld device when we go
in through the door, and the moment we leave. That way it is noted
exactly how long the visit has lasted,' explains Pia, a public-sector
care-giver to the elderly, explaining how a shift in working practices
in Copenhagen has transformed her work.

Previously, her visits to the elderly were planned, broken down into
different tasks with a specific time allotment for each task. Eye drops
(five minutes), help to use the toilet (ten minutes), help to get up
and to eat (ten minutes). There were seventy individual tasks, and
the clock would be ticking.

'All the time, you were working with the handheld computer and
focusing on how long the specific tasks should take.'

In 2011, the city of Copenhagen ran a pilot project to test how a trust-based system would work, compared to 'the minute tyranny', as it was called. Instead of spending time on entering the things you'd done, the time should be spent helping the person you were looking after. Instead of being told what to do and how long it should take, the employee should figure out what to do, in collaboration with the person they were caring for.

'We should not control the employees. It is the care-givers who have the insight to evaluate what is needed during the visit,' said Mayor Ninna Thomsen.

The pilot project was a huge success. It didn't cause an increase in expenditure, and employee satisfaction soared. It has now been spread to the care-giving sector across the entire district and has led to the trust reform of the public sector in Copenhagen. The city is now shifting its focus away from rules, bureaucracy and reporting requirements to the question of what is best for citizens and how each employee can deliver greatest value. Managers and employees are assessed on the basis of feedback from citizens rather than through processes, monitoring and reports.

'Today, there is a belief that we can evaluate what the senior citizen needs,' explains Pia, who now experiences greater work satisfaction. She is not alone. Employee satisfaction has risen, and sick days are down. 'Before, you did what you had been told to do – and then you rushed out the door. Today, you can focus the service on the client, provide it if they need something else. Today, it is more free.'

HAPPINESS TIP:
TURN COMPETITION INTO COOPERATION

Change games of competition into games of cooperation by reconfiguring rules and goals.

In order to teach our kids the value and fun of cooperation over competition, perhaps we could tweak some classic games. We all know the game musical chairs, right? Ten kids; nine chairs; when the music stops you find a chair; if you don't find one, you are out; one chair is removed each round, until there are two people and only one chair. So, basically, a mild version of *Hunger Games* for people who *really* like to sit.

This game also teaches our kids how to fight over scarce resources. And if you are one of the first to go out, you get to stand and watch the game instead of taking part. FUN! How about we turn it into a game of cooperation? We still start with ten kids and nine chairs but, when the music stops, we all sit – two kids share one chair. Well done. Now, we remove one chair but all the kids stay in the game. The music stops, and this time two chairs must seat two kids each. You get the picture. At the end, all ten kids try and fit on one chair together. Instead of teaching them how to compete, we teach them how to cooperate.

FIVE WAYS TO ENCOURAGE EMPATHY IN KIDS

———

1. **WALK AND NARRATE:** Go for a walk and look for someone in a grey jacket (or whatever you decide). Once you have identified such a person, spend the rest of the walk talking about what you imagine their life is like, based on how they look.

2. **DRAW:** Draw a face in the middle of a sheet of paper expressing joy, anger, sorrow or some other emotion, then draw what would make the person feel like that.

3. **PLAY:** 'Feeling of the Week': Select a feeling, draw or write it on a Post-it and stick it on the fridge. Then, all week, ask your child to point out this particular feeling when they spot it in themselves or in others.

4. **GESTURES:** Stand in front of a mirror. Put your arms behind your back and talk, then use your arms to make gestures expressing what you were saying. (This can also be played with two people, where one does the talking and the other the gestures.)

5. **MUTE:** Play one of your kids' favourite films but with the sound off. Talk about the facial expressions you see, what they mean and why the characters may feel this way.

THE ARMS RACE:
BEAUTY AND BRAINS

*'What are you here for today?' the picture-perfect
receptionist asks me.*

To fully understand the importance of trust and cooperation, we
need to visit one of the most competitive countries.

I am in Seoul – the plastic surgery capital of the world – in Gangnam
district, which is also known as the Improvement Quarter or the
Beauty Belt because of the five hundred clinics here (including
Cinderella, Reborn and the Centre for Human Appearance). The
clinic I am standing in is seventeen storeys tall and there is a Ferrari
parked right in front of the entrance. It's red. Obviously.

'M-my my ear,' I stutter. 'It looks like someone took a bite out of it. I
want to have it fixed.'

The first part is true. The second part isn't. I am happy with my ear.
It earned me the nickname Evander Holyfield in high school and,
for a guy who wears tweed, glasses and elbow patches on a regular
basis, it was the closest I ever came to having a bad-boy image.

The real reason I am here is to understand what you could call the
beauty arms race.

Estimates based on statistics from the International Society of Aesthetic Plastic Surgery indicate that one in fifty have turned to the knife or the needle in Korea, putting the country in first position on a per capita basis: twenty procedures per thousand people, compared with thirteen per thousand in the US. The UK is not included in these statistics, but data from the British Association of Aesthetic Plastic Surgeons found that 51,140 procedures were carried out in 2015, which would put the UK at around 0.8 procedures per thousand people.

However, it has been suggested that the numbers in Korea may be considerably higher, as procedures which take place at private clinics may not be registered – some reports say that 20 per cent of the female population has had plastic surgery at least once in their lives, while others claim as many as 50 per cent of women under the age of thirty have undergone cosmetic surgery in Seoul.

Whatever the exact number may be, it leaves us with the same question: Why are the numbers so high?

First, with surgery prices in Seoul at around a third of what you would pay in the US, surgery tourists make up a part of the statistic. Package deals are offered, hotels are attached to clinics so clients do not have to walk through the streets in bandages and, indeed, suitcases fill the lobby of the clinic in which I am standing. Second, double-eyelid surgery (an insertion of a crease in the eyelid to make the eye look bigger) is popular here and is a simple procedure which can take as little as fifteen minutes (the former President of Korea, Roh Moo-hyun, had it done in 2005 while in office). Which brings us to reason three: men do it, too, making up 15–20 per cent of the clients.

In the Seoul metro, you may be greeted with cosmetic surgery adverts claiming that 'Everyone but you has done it.' And that leads us to the fourth reason. Competition.

Remember the Korean saying, 'If one cousin buys land, the other cousin gets a stomach ache.' First, your neighbour bought a new car, then you bought a new car. Now the competition has moved into different arenas: beauty and education.

'Korea is a very competitive society,' Yeon-Ho says to me.

He and I have met a couple of times before. The first time was at my office in Copenhagen, when he was doing research for a book on why Denmark does so well in the happiness rankings and what Korea could learn from it. Now we are in Seoul, and we meet in the centre of the city as thousands and thousands of demonstrators protest against President Park over the corruption scandal (which later leads to her being impeached and removed from office).

'We need to give the Korean students a break from competition. That is why I started the Danish *efterskole* here.'

Students in South Korea are the most hardworking I have ever met. The ones I speak with start the first school (yes, the first school) at 8 a.m. and finish at 4 p.m., then they go home to eat. The second school can last from 6 p.m. until 9 p.m., and can be lessons from a private tutor or a *hagwons* (a for-profit private cram school). Three quarters of students attend such a 'second school'. *Hagwons* and private tutors are big business and serve to accelerate the academic arms race to get into one of the three most prestigious universities in South Korea – Seoul National University, Korea University and Yonsei University (also known as SKY) – and subsequently on the pathway to a job in one of the top companies.

The exam that determines which university you go to is obviously a big deal and, when it takes place, everything seems to revolve around it. The country's stock market opens an hour later and office hours are changed to reduce morning traffic so students do not risk being delayed. According to National Statistics Korea, more than half of children between the ages of fifteen and nineteen who are suicidal give 'academic performance and college entrance' as a reason. In 2008, the competition became so fierce that the government put a curfew on *hagwons* and private tutoring: No more school after 10 p.m. Citizens were paid bounties to turn in anyone who violated the rule; patrols controlled *hagwons* and made raids and busts. 'Everybody be cool – this is a police raid: put down your books!'

It is hard to argue with Yeon-Ho's point about giving the students a break, and that is why the first thing he took back to Korea from Denmark was the concept of an *efterskole*.

His dream for the school is to give the students the experience of being a small society where they take responsibility for their own life. Where they experience a sense of community and happiness and focus on things other than studying for an exam. Where they learn to cooperate rather than compete.

'That is why I tell the students, if something does not go according to plan, you will still succeed in your stay, because you will learn a great deal on the way. By being in company with yourself and with each other – and by being happy.'

This way of raising kids puts greater focus on togetherness, trust, empathy and cooperation. In short, social skills. The aim is not to create a human robot with the highest possible efficiency but to shape a person who understands and helps other people.

TIGER MUMS OR ELEPHANT MUMS

Not everyone agrees with the educational system in Denmark or the way Danish kids are raised. In 2011, the book Battle Hymn of the Tiger Mother *appeared to be the anti-manifesto to the Danish way of bringing up children.*

The book seemed to advocate putting on the pressure to achieve academic excellence, restrictions or outright bans on extracurricular and social activities like sleepovers (so, essentially, an embargo on fun) and punishment and the embedding of a feeling of shame if the kids failed to live up to their parents' high expectations.

In 2013, a study by Professor Su Yeong Kim, an associate professor in human development and family sciences at the University of Texas, shed light on the effect of tiger-mumness. According to Professor Kim, tiger cubs got worse grades, felt more depressed and more alienated from their parents than the kids of parents whom their kids characterized as 'supportive' or 'easy-going'.

A few years after the Tiger mother's battle hymn, the author, Chua – the original tiger mum – and her husband were asked in the course of an interview with the *Guardian* about why some cultural groups get ahead in the US. Chua explained that their approach had been to look at measures of income in the US census, but pointed out that this was a 'very materialistic sense of success, but we're not saying this is the only way – this doesn't mean happiness, you know?' Her husband also had some concerns about high demands being placed on people.

'I know that I am unhappier,' he said, 'because I always feel like whatever I've done is not good enough. It doesn't matter what I do – so that's painful, and I worry that I've communicated that to my kids.'

There is no perfect parenting method, just as there is no perfect parent and no perfect kid. We all try our best. But let's take a look now at the benefits of the path of elephant mums and dads – parents who nurture and encourage their children, and believe that, if a child knows that they are loved – and not because of their marks in school – that love will give them the strength to find and follow their own way towards happiness.

I was fortunate enough to be raised by elephants. Had it not been for my parents' encouragement to do what makes me happy – and them letting me know that I was loved, wherever life would take me – I am not sure I would have had the courage to start a journey in which failure was a likely outcome but which instead has brought me happiness and taken me on adventures around the world.

On one of these adventures, I met a violinist who had been raised by a tiger mum. In third grade, I was put in the corner in music class by a substitute teacher who thought I was deliberately trying to ruin the singing lesson. I wasn't. I just have no musical sense whatsoever. No tiger mum could have changed that. In any case, the violinist and I were both speaking at an event in London, and we got talking about how differently we had been raised. 'When I was a kid, my mother asked me what I wanted to be when I grew up,' she told me.

'I want to be happy,' she had answered. 'Don't be foolish,' her mother had replied. 'That is not a real ambition.' That day in London, she played the violin. It was the most impressive display of musical skills I had ever heard.

I am sure her mother was happy. I hope she was, too.

MILE-HIGH HIERARCHY

In countries with more economic equality, the percentage of people agreeing that 'most people can be trusted' is higher.

The same goes for individual US states – the more economically equal the state is, the more people trust each other. If we trust each other, we feel safe and have less to worry about – and we tend to see others as cooperators rather than competitors.

Trust levels are not static and, in countries like the UK and the US, they have fallen. For half a century, wealth has increased in the US, but inequality has soared, causing trust to go into free fall.

Inequality leads to mistrust, competition, resentment and anger. It is on the rise globally and, while we used to experience an 'elevator effect', rich and poor rising and falling as one, poorer people now feel left behind. And with growing inequality, more and more people will feel left out, scared and angry.

The maladies of inequality are nicely summed up in *The Spirit Level – Why Equality is Better for Everyone* by Richard G. Wilkinson, professor of social epidemiology at the University of Nottingham, and Kate Picket, professor of epidemiology in the department of health sciences at the University of York. A high level of inequality reduces empathy, trust and both physical and mental health and leads to more violence, higher crime rates, more obesity and teenage births.

However, I think one of the most interesting studies to disembark the cabin recently (2015) is one by Katherine DeCelles and Michael Norton which examined instances of 'air rage'.

Air rage is unruly or violent behaviour on the part of a passenger caused by physiological and psychological stresses associated with air travel. It includes acting in a threatening manner to the staff, removing your trousers and sitting in your boxers for the entire flight . . . one person even tried to choke the passenger in front of him because that person had leaned his seat back.

What the two professors (from Harvard Business School and the University of Toronto, respectively) examined was not only whether, for instance, the size of the individual seats or delays correlated with air rage, but also the class structure in these microcosms of society – in other words, inequality.

They found that physical inequality – the presence of a first-class cabin – on an aeroplane is associated with more frequent air rage back in economy class. Passengers in economy class were almost four times more likely to choke the guy in front of them if they were on a plane with a first-class section. In fact, according to the authors of the study, the presence of first-class has the same or an even bigger effect on the odds of air rage as a nine-and-a-half-hour flight delay.

But it is not only the economy passengers that are behaving badly. When people from a higher social class are more aware of their upper-class status, they are more likely to engage in antisocial behaviour, to be less compassionate and to feel that they are entitled. Or, to use the scientific term for individuals engaging in antisocial behaviour: 'assholes'.

In addition – and here is where I think it gets fascinating – the study found that the economy passengers who had to walk through first class to get to their seat were more likely to express air rage.

Broadly speaking, you can board from the front, the middle or the back of the plane – and only boarding from the front will send you through the section where you can witness what you get in first class. Seeing the free champagne, the fully reclining seats and the smug smiles on the faces of the first-class passengers made people travelling in economy two times more likely to put their hands around somebody's throat.

Other factors, such as the size of the individual seats, seem not to matter. The study demonstrates the importance of considering not just the design of aeroplanes, offices and stadiums in understanding and preventing antisocial behaviour but also the design of our societies when it comes to inequality.

In many ways, the UK is a pioneer in the well-being field. For one thing, the Annual Population Survey asks 160,000 people every year four well-being questions such as 'Overall, how happy did you feel yesterday?', 'Overall, how satisfied are you with your life nowadays?', 'Overall, how anxious did you feel yesterday?' and 'Overall, to what extent do you feel the things you do in your life are worthwhile?' That gives nerds like me a good opportunity to understand what can explain why some people voted to leave the EU and why some people wanted to remain in the Brexit referendum.

According to the New Economic Foundation, happiness inequality was a strong predictor of an area voting to leave the EU. The biggest happiness gaps were found in places like Blaenau Gwent in the Welsh valleys, where an overwhelming majority voted to leave, while the lowest inequality in well-being turned out to be in places like Cheshire East and Falkirk, which were vastly in favour of remaining. On average, in the twenty most unequal places in Britain in terms of well-being, 57 per cent of voters wanted to leave, while in the twenty most equal places, only 43 per cent voted to leave.

Three months before the Brexit vote, the World Happiness Report pointed out that inequality in well-being has a stronger negative impact on well-being than income inequalities and, as the New Economic Foundation pointed out, *income* inequality was not at all associated with voting to leave but *well-being* inequality was. This supports the case that our subjective feelings about our life and the comparisons we make of it with that of others are a better predictor of whether people are dissatisfied and feeling left behind. We get angry when we are faced with inequality – and we are not alone: in fact, we are wired to react to inequality and injustice.

Inequality in Well-being

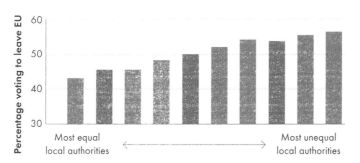

LET THEM EAT GRAPES

If I had to do something other than my job, I would opt for Frans de Waal's job. He's a primatologist and studies the social behaviour of monkeys.

His book _Chimpanzee Politics_ argued that the roots of politics are older than humanity (although it seems that, in recent years, human politicians have become more likely to throw faeces at each other). However, his work also argues that we might be physically wired to react strongly to inequality.

De Waal has studied how capuchin monkeys react to inequality by pairing them and having them both perform the same task – giving the researcher a stone. In return for the stone, the first monkey receives a piece of cucumber, is happy with that and so will go on handing the researcher stones in exchange for it – until the moment when it sees the second monkey get a grape, which monkeys prefer over cucumber, in exchange for the stone.

The first monkey tries again, tests the rock this time by hitting it against the wall, hands it to the researcher and in return is again handed a piece of cucumber. Then the tantrum sets in. The monkey rattles the cage, pounds the floor and throws the cucumber back at the researcher.

I once mentioned to my brother that we could test De Waal's findings by giving my youngest nephew two chocolate biscuits, then giving his older brother one. Since then, for some reason, I have not been asked to babysit.

The point of all this is that while we can improve trust levels in the short term by training our empathy muscles and teaching our kids to cooperate rather than compete, there is something we need to address in the long term to improve trust and happiness. And this is the understanding that my happiness also depends not only on how my family are but also on how my neighbours' children fare. It is honouring the noble principle that I am the keeper of my brothers and sisters – and they are mine. And it is judging our societies not by the success of those who finish first but how we lift back up those who fall.

Read literary fiction and move beyond your normal social circles to get a better understanding of other people's behaviour.

Put yourself in the shoes of others and pick up some literary fiction. Go for books like *To Kill a Mockingbird* by Harper Lee, *The Great Gatsby* by F. Scott Fitzgerald or *The Grapes of Wrath* by John Steinbeck. Find social blenders that allow you to move beyond your normal social circles. Visit places that voted in the opposite end of the political spectrum from you. If you listen to people's stories, you may find that you might have made some of the same choices if you had lived their life rather than yours. We are not so very different; we just had different starting points. And while it is easy to stop listening and dismiss people we disagree with as ignorant, as evil and as the enemy, that will only lead us to misery. But perhaps if we listen we might learn that it is inequality, unfairness and injustice that are the enemy and that empathy, trust and cooperation are the way forward.

T R U S T

The 'lost wallet' experiment

Helsinki, Finland: Researchers 'dropped' wallets in different cities. Each wallet contained a name, a mobile phone number, a family photo, coupons, business cards and the equivalent of $50. In Helsinki, 92 per cent of the wallets were returned with the money still inside them. Read more on pp. 204–205.

Parallel Narrative Experience

Israel and Palestine: The Parents' Circle Families Forum is a grassroots organization of Palestinian and Israeli families who have lost immediate family members in the conflict. A process called the Parallel Narrative Experience aims to help each side of the conflict understand the personal and national narratives of the other. The members meet with one another on a regular basis in order to forge mutual understanding and respect between the communities.

Cooperation and empathy through Live Action Roleplaying

Østerskov, Denmark: Østerskov efterskole use Live Action Roleplaying to teach the kids; perhaps pupils spend a week in ancient Rome or on Wall Street. The teachers find that, for instance, children with Asperger's learn social skills and how to handle social situations by playing different characters in the games.

From custodians of prisoners to captains of life

Singapore: The Singapore Prison Service has changed its prisons into schools for life by focusing on cooperation and rehabilitation. Prison officers have been assigned to manage all matters relating to the inmates in a particular housing unit, and they take on the role of mentor and counsellor. The inmates are given the power to make decisions, as long as these serve to help them make a change for the better. By any measure, the results have been impressive, ranging from improved staff morale and safety, better social connections between prisons and the rest of society and a drop in recidivism from 44 to 27 per cent over a ten-year period.

Favela Painting Foundation

Rio de Janeiro, Brazil: In the favelas of Rio de Janeiro, artists have created a small, but significant, revolution. And their main weapons are a brush and some colourful paint. In an open, collaborative and inclusive process, they paint the favela houses in the colours of the rainbow – and a lot of local young people help with the project, making it theirs. They choose the colours together, paint together and play together. Today, it is a new world that greets the locals and the tourists. It is bright, colourful and proud. These are not just houses, these are homes. And the people who live here are now proud to call it their home, and they are proud to show that they have more to offer the world than the world might have expected.

CHAPTER EIGHT

KINDNESS

KINDNESS

One of the most inspiring people I have met on my journeys is a man I'm going to call Clark. That is not his real name (his identity is a secret) and he is the closest thing to a superhero you can get.

Clark has sat next to Tim on planes purely to help him get over his fear of flying. He has helped Anthony raise awareness of the lack of disabled access in the London Underground. He has reunited a lost memory card with its owner and tried to do the same to a son and his long-lost father. All were complete strangers.

His superpower: kindness. Clark is otherwise known as the Free Help Guy.

'When we are growing up, I think we all dream of changing the world, but in my late twenties I found myself going to work every day, commuting to Oxford Circus station, together with thousands of other people. It was a good job, but I wasn't changing the world.

'I just got to this point where I was doing things that didn't seem to have any kind of meaning. Commuting, working and struggling with it. Just feeling a bit lost. I imagined myself five years down the line, doing the same thing, and had that feeling that somehow it didn't feel right. So I quit.'

Clark made a promise to himself to spend six months not working. He still wanted to earn, but he wanted to earn a value that was measured in things other than notes and coins.

He spent the first week watching *Breaking Bad*. But then he decided to post a note on the internet. 'If you need help, I'll help. For free. (Especially if your needs are fun, different and morally deserved.) TheFreeHelpGuy.'

He had a reply within the day.

'I decided I wanted to help people. But I wanted to be hands on, I wanted it to be personal, and I wanted to have a bit of freedom with it as well.'

The first reply was from Jill and Richard, a couple living on the south coast in England, in Plymouth. The year before, they had given their spare room to a homeless man, 'He's now got a job and has rented his own place,' they wrote. 'Can you help find us someone else to help?'

Later came Vince, an IT manager who wanted to be a stage hypnotist and needed a guinea pig; and Sophie, who asked for help in naming her baby. Clark suggested Zeus. The parents went in a different direction.

Then came Jill from America, who asked for help to reunite her husband, Ian, with his long-lost father, Frank, who lived in the UK. It turned out Frank had died, and Clark had to phone to tell Ian, someone he had never met, that his father was no longer alive. Not the happy ending we had all hoped for, but at least now Ian knew.

There was Margot, a young girl who suffered from leukaemia and needed help to find a bone-marrow donor. Clark organized eighty people into a 'help mob' which dropped flyers around a local swabbing centre to find suitable donors. Margot found a donor, but her life could not be saved. Sadly, she died ten months later.

Helping people, listening to their stories and getting involved in their hopes and dreams and struggles bring both sorrow and satisfaction. When we get to know people, we start to care more. We take part in their victories – and share their defeats. Life is messy, and relationships are hard. The outcome of helping may be a mixed bag. Getting involved also means that we can get hurt from time to time.

But helping also brings a sense of purpose.

Eden, who was nine when Clark first met her and her mother, Trudy, has myoclonus diaphragmatic flutter. It is also known as belly dancer's syndrome; a misfiring diaphragm causes spasms throughout the body, preventing speech and triggering seizures. It is such a rare condition that Eden is the only sufferer in the UK. The only specialist in the world was thousands of kilometres away – in Colorado, in the US. So Clark raised the £4,000 needed for flights, accommodation and initial consultations in Colorado through crowdfunding and by harassing journalists.

When I meet Clark in 2015, Eden is 'doing really well'. For someone who wanted to earn a value that was measured in non-monetary ways, he seems to have found a new currency, one that is easily converted into happiness.

'I think people have that assumption that London is expensive and you've got to focus on earning. But I think you can still find the time to help.' However, the most common request Clark gets is 'Can I help you?' People want to help.

Helping has also changed Clark's life. 'My heart beats in a way that it never has. My life is vivid. Giving is happiness. The person who has been helped the most by this free help project is me,' he says. He now works as a freelance business consultant, but has dropped the six-month time frame he gave himself at first and now wants to help for life, and he hopes the Free Help Guy will be kept alive after he is gone.

HAPPINESS TIP:
BE MORE AMÉLIE

Find ways to bring happiness to others through acts of kindness.

In the movie *Amélie*, the shy waitress finds an old metal box of childhood memorabilia that has been hidden by a boy who lived in her apartment decades earlier. Amélie finds the boy – now a grown man – and returns the box to him. She promises herself that, if it makes him happy, she will devote her life to bringing happiness to others. The man is moved to tears, and Amélie embarks on her new mission. She starts a romance between people. She persuades her father to follow his dream of touring the world. She escorts a blind man to the Métro station, giving a rich description of the street scenes they pass. I think, the world needs more Amélies. What if we all became secret superheroes of kindness?

FIVE RANDOM ACTS OF KINDNESS TO DO THIS WEEK

1. LEAVE A GIFT ON SOMEONE'S DOORSTEP.

2. LEARN THE NAME OF THE PERSON AT THE FRONT DESK, OR SOMEONE ELSE YOU SEE EVERY DAY. GREET THEM BY NAME.

3. MAKE TWO LUNCHES AND GIVE ONE AWAY.

4. TALK TO THE SHY PERSON WHO'S BY THEMSELVES AT A PARTY OR AT THE OFFICE.

5. GIVE SOMEONE A GENUINE COMPLIMENT. RIGHT NOW.

HELPER'S HIGH: FEELING GOOD BY DOING GOOD

There is a Chinese proverb that goes

> *'If you want happiness for an hour –
> take a nap. If you want happiness for
> a day – go fishing. If you want happiness
> for a year – inherit a fortune. If you
> want happiness for a lifetime – help
> someone else.'*

Altruism is concern for the welfare of others and it is one of the factors that explains why some countries are happier than others. According to the World Happiness Report 2012, a society cannot be happy unless there is a high degree of altruism among its members.

However, it is not just society in general that becomes happier through altruism. We feel personally better. Try to recall a time you did something nice for a stranger, not because you wanted to gain something from it, just for the pure purpose of helping somebody else. How did that action make you feel?

For me, it was something as simple as giving someone a banana. Walking home from the supermarket, I was waiting at a red light. Next to me was a mother with her kid, who was crying: 'I am hungry.'

It was a quick fix. I broke one of the bananas I had bought off the bunch and handed it to the mother: 'Would you like a banana for your kid?' I had seldom seen anyone so grateful. She was happy. The kid was happy. I was happy. Here we are talking about affective happiness – our mood. My happiness was in part caused by helper's high.

The term is based on the theory that doing something good makes us feel good, because the action produces a mild version of a morphine high. Our brain has something called the nucleus accumbens – also known as the reward centre – which is activated in response to food or sex.

Neurological research from the National Institutes of Health under the US Department of Health and Human Services finds that the area of our brain that is activated in response to food or pleasure also lights up when participants in the study think about giving money to charity. In other words, we are wired to feel good when we do something that makes our species survive. Cooperating is good for the survival of our species, so we are wired to feel good when we engage in it.

HAPPINESS TIP:
CELEBRATE WORLD KINDNESS DAY

Get your friends together and get creative on how you can celebrate kindness.

What better way to celebrate World Kindness Day than with kindness? World Kindness Day was introduced by the World Kindness Movement, a group of national kindness organizations, in 1998 and is celebrated on 13 November each year. In the UK, there is also a National Kindness Day – this year it was held on 31 March.

Get your friends together and form a 'help mob' (a helpful flash mob), say, for a charity or somebody who needs a hand with something; dress up as a superhero and perform random acts of kindness that day; or call or write to someone who has been kind to you in the past and thank them.

GIVE YOUR TIME

Not only can our current mood be improved by a helper's high, but altruism can also affect our overall happiness and how we evaluate our lives.

People who volunteer are happier than those who do not, even after controlling for other factors such as socioeconomic status. Moreover, they experience fewer depressive symptoms, less anxiety and enjoy a more meaningful life. Part of the explanation may be that people who are happier tend to be more inclined to sign up for voluntary work. However, another part may also be that some groups may expose you to the way in which people who are less fortunate than you live and thus make you more grateful for what you have. Doing voluntary work may also have indirect positive effects.

When I was twenty-three I volunteered as a youth counsellor for the Red Cross. During the introductory course, we were told about jobs other than that of counsellor that were available. There was one that involved going around to high schools and giving presentations on teenage issues, empathy and how to be a good listener, and a PR group, which worked on communications. I started being vocally enthusiastic about the first group – but as more and more people seemed to become interested in it I started to speak positively about the PR group. A girl sitting next to me leaned in and whispered, 'Let me guess. You want to join the presentation group, and you became worried that it would fill up. So you started promoting the PR group. Well played.' Frederikke and I have now been friends for fifteen years.

There are two points to this story. First, doing voluntary work is a great way to meet new friends – and second, always make friends with people who can see through you. Studies back up my experience that volunteering can lead to more social relationships and friendships, and this (I hope this comes as no surprise at this point) has an impact on our happiness.

It may also be one of the reasons for the large number of Danes who engage in voluntary work. At the time of writing, 42 per cent of Danes are engaged in unpaid activities and 70 per cent have been active in the last five years, according to the Danish Institute for Voluntary Effort – and this helps to keep Denmark happy.

The question, of course, remains: if kindness is so great, why aren't we doing more of it? If there is a helper's high, why aren't rock stars checking into rehab centres because they volunteer too much?

According to a report by Jill Loga of the Norwegian Institute for Social Research, perhaps the reason is that most of us see volunteering as doing something good for others – not for ourselves. In other words, we need to highlight the personal benefits that come from perpetrating acts of kindness and altruism, such as getting more friends and making us feel more grateful for what we have. You don't have to sign up to do work for a charity, it could be anything from volunteering to help out at football practice to simply giving out more smiles to strangers in the street.

CASE STUDY
SOPHIE

'Looking back, I may have had depression or something.'

As a result of the financial crisis, Sophie was made redundant. 'I had been used to working at full speed. I loved my work, but I also had all these ideas of what I would do if I had the time. The irony was that, when I lost my job, I couldn't seem to get out of bed.'

In the following months, she felt she lost who she was and had been. 'My job was my identity – that was gone. My social network was my colleagues. Gone – or not gone – but gone awkward. We used to talk about work – and now I wasn't part of that conversation.'

She started to isolate herself. She found going to dinner parties the worst; everybody would be talking about their careers, and how busy they were. 'Or you would chat with someone, and then the dreaded question would come: "So what do you do?" I developed a sense of when that question would be approaching and would quickly excuse myself.

'It became tiring.' Then came the period she calls 'doubt and out'.

'My self-esteem took a nosedive. Being made redundant was one thing. But the stream of rejections in the job hunt made me question myself and doubt my own abilities. I started to think I had just been faking it all these years and they had called my bluff – and now I was out for good.'

Months later, she was still out of a job. Then, one Sunday, her sister phoned. 'My sister volunteers and had pastries for a cake sale in her apartment, but she had to take her son to A and E.' She asked Sophie, who lived close by, to fetch the pastries and go to the cake sale in her place.

'She had asked me to join her at the sale on numerous occasions, and I had always said no, but that afternoon I felt like me again for the first time in a long time. I had fun. I felt useful. I had worked in the events business, so I was like a fish in the water.

'I remembered who I was – and I was not faking it. I managed the shit out of that cake sale.' She laughs. She started joining her sister in her voluntary work. 'It became my way back, I think. It was voluntary work, so there were no demands. I could do it at my own pace.'

Today, she is back working in the events business – someone attending the cake sales spotted her talent for organization – but Sophie continues to work as a volunteer. 'My identity has two legs to stand on now, I see my sister more often – and there is cake.'

HAPPINESS TIP:
VOLUNTEER

Find ways you can volunteer to help others. Improve your community and develop your sense of purpose.

Whether it's a one-off or something you do every week, volunteering is good all round. You are making your local community happier, increasing your trust in others and theirs in you, improving your skills and meeting new people who may turn into friends.

Volunteering comes in many forms, and you may want to combine it with some of your personal goals and interests:

- Passionate about politics? Volunteer to do some work for a local candidate you feel positive about.
- Need training in public speaking? Find a teaching role and share some of your expertise.
- Interested in learning more about foreign cultures? Become a mentor for an expat.
- Love the outdoors? Environmental organizations need your help to maintain nature trails.
- Want more exercise? Do some coaching.
- Want to gain practice in playing music in front of an audience? Contact local organizations that care for the elderly.

Browse portals of volunteer opportunities. In the UK, you can visit do-it.org, which lists more than a million options and enables 200,000 people to donate their time and build their skills every month.

Still not sure? Then go for a one-day test drive. Take a friend. Or find one there.

'RESTING BITCH FACE' NATION?

──────

Because Denmark often does well in the happiness rankings, you would expect Danes to be walking around with blissful smiles on their faces.

That is not always the case. Danish men and women have been accused of suffering from RBF (resting bitch face) or having a zombie death stare. Despite being happy, Danes do not necessarily look kind and friendly.

Danes will often say that they notice, when they go away on holiday, other people smile more. At the same time, people from London tell me that they find the Danes smile a lot. So, who is right? Do Danes smile more or less than other people?

In order to be able to answer that question, I started to collect data three years ago. In most of the cities I've visited in the past few years I have measured the frequency of smiles. At the Happiness Research Institute, we now have more than thirty thousand data points in more than twenty cities around the world. Not exactly work per se – more like an expensive hobby. But how do you measure the frequency of smiles? Basically, I do what I guess you also enjoy doing when visiting cities. Sit down at a café, have a coffee and look at people.

But I needed to be random in the people I observed; otherwise, my attention might be drawn to women in bright red dresses or people talking loudly. So I would say to myself, 'OK, the first person who comes around that corner, or the first person who steps on that manhole in the pavement, that is the one I'll watch.'

After observing the person for five seconds (without them noticing; that would influence the result), I note down whether they smile or not, their gender, estimate their age, jot down whether they are with someone or not and what they are doing. Are they drinking coffee, talking on the telephone, walking their dog, or what?

I have watched thousands and thousands of people going about their daily business, hundreds and hundreds speaking on the phone, dozens and dozens holding hands – and one guy picking his nose.

Apart from the distribution of smiles among people, you start to notice other patterns when you examine the data you've collected. Italian couples are more inclined to hold hands, regardless of age, Mexicans are more likely to be snacking on something, and you see dog walkers more frequently in Paris and Vancouver.

The biggest challenge is, of course, to register only locals and weed out the tourists. The guy with the camera and the map and a confused look on his face is probably not from around here. And you can be fairly certain that the woman with her hands full of groceries pacing by the Duomo Cathedral in Milan without looking up is likely to be a local.

So, do Danes smile more than anyone in the world? No, people in Milan smile just as much, and people in Málaga smile even more than Danes. However, people in Copenhagen smile more than people in New York, Marrakesh and Warsaw. On average, 12.7 per cent of people smile in Copenhagen, less than 2 per cent in New York, and people in Málaga smile more frequently (almost 14 per cent).

However, this should all be taken with a pinch of salt, because what matters is whether people are with others. People seldom smile when they are by themselves; this is something that's common across the countries I've visited.

There is a strong link between whether people walk alone or with other people and how often people smile. In cities like New York, Seoul and Riga, people usually walk by themselves in the daytime. Fewer than one in five is with someone else – and the smile ratio in these countries is among the lowest in the world. At the other end of the spectrum are smiling cities like Málaga and Milan, where people are more often with others.

Therefore, it also matters *where* in the city you measure smiles. You will get a higher frequency of smiles in Regent's Park where friends and family stroll together than on the busy Strand in central London.

How often do people smile on the streets?

1st	2nd	3rd
Málaga	Milan	Kuala Lumpur
13.9%	**12.7%**	**12.5%**

Copenhagen: **12.7%**

Madrid: **9.5%**

Montreal: **9.5%**

Guadalajara: **9.2%**

Stockholm: **9.2%**

Lisbon: **7.7%**

Riga: **7.1%**

Marrakesh: **6.8%**

Vancouver: **6.8%**

Warsaw: **6.2%**

Paris: **5.1%**

Helsinki: **4.7%**

Seoul: **4.7%**

Amsterdam: **4.4%**

London: **4.3%**

Dublin: **4%**

Lille: **3.3%**

New York: **1.4%**

Source: The Happiness Research Institute

Culture also comes into play. In some countries, smiling people may be perceived as kinder, friendlier and more attractive, while in others smiling is associated with lower levels of intelligence.

A team of researchers led by Kuba Krys, a psychologist at the Polish Academy of Sciences, has gained some insight into cultural differences in the perception of smiling individuals. The researchers asked 4,519 participants from 44 different cultures to rate photos of smiling and unsmiling individuals on how honest and intelligent they thought these individuals were.

Countries to the left of the red line to the left consider smiling people to be significantly less intelligent than non-smiling individuals; countries to the right of the red line to the right rate people who smile as significantly more intelligent.

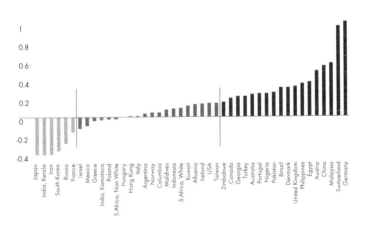

Source: Kuba Krys et al, 'Be Careful Where You Smile: Culture Shapes Judgements of Intelligence and Honesty of Smiling Individuals', Journal of Nonverbal Behavior, 2016

The researchers found that in countries like Germany, Switzerland and Malaysia, smiling people were perceived as significantly more intelligent than people who didn't smile, while in countries like Japan, South Korea and Russia, people who smiled were perceived as less intelligent. In fact, I've been told there is a Russian proverb that translates as 'Laughing for no reason is a sign of stupidity.'

HAPPINESS TIP:
SMILE AND CHAT TO STRANGERS

Hand out smiles and friendly remarks. They are free.

Make small talk. Have a friendly chat. Give a compliment. Americans have mastered this art; Danes are notoriously bad at friendly chats with strangers.

I try to be better at it, but sometimes I try and I fail. Two years ago, I walked into a lift at a university in Copenhagen. In it was a man who looked very much like me and dressed exactly like me: glasses, brown leather briefcase, blue trousers, white shirt, brown blazer. Also like me, his longish hair was going grey – or, as I like to call it, executive blond. Anyway, he looked like my stunt double – elbow patches and all.

'Are you here for the twin study, too?' I asked.

'No.'

Longest lift ride ever.

Sometimes you swing for kindness but awkwardness hits you in the face. But sometimes you try and you succeed and, for those five seconds, the world is a better place. It may also be the first five seconds of a longer journey towards a kinder world. Remember, big things often have small beginnings.

KINDNESS: A LANGUAGE THAT THE BLIND CAN SEE

—————

Mark Twain once wrote that kindness is a language which the deaf can hear and the blind can see. Robert Levine has taken that literally.

One day when he was six years old he saw a man lying in the middle of a crowded pavement in a busy part of New York City. The people passing by were not only ignoring the man but were avoiding getting too close to him.

Many years later, travelling in Myanmar, Robert found himself in a crowded market in Rangoon. The sun was hot, the air was dusty and it was difficult to breathe. Suddenly, a young man carrying a huge bag fell down in the middle of the crowd. People quickly gathered around him. Sellers left their stands, brought him water and placed a blanket under his head while they fetched a doctor.

Today, Robert is a professor of psychology at California State University and is researching what makes people care for each other and why cities are so different when it comes to their approach to kindness. Robert has conducted three different experiments, all on busy streets, to test the kindness of strangers.

The experiments involve creating a situation in which a stranger needs help. In the pen scenario, a pen is dropped on the pavement, apparently without its owner noticing. In the hurt scenario, an experimenter wearing a leg brace and walking with a limp drops a magazine and is obviously struggling to pick it up. In the blind scenario, the experimenter feigns blindness and approaches the kerb of a busy junction and waits for someone to help him cross the street.

What the researchers discovered was that the main predictor of how much people help others in cities is how crowded the city is. If there are more people, individuals feel more disconnected and less responsible for others and are therefore less willing to help. When they looked at twenty-four cities in the US, the researchers found that the lowest level of help was in New York City and the highest was in Knoxville, Tennessee.

Nevertheless, Rio de Janeiro in Brazil turned out to be the place with the kindest people on earth – more helpful than those in Copenhagen, for example – even though Rio has about twelve times more citizens than the Danish capital. (One curious thing: Copenhagen is a city where people are more likely to pick up a pen than to help a blind person across the street. The reason for this might be that Danes put a high price on personal space – or pens.) So why is there so much kindness in such a crowded place as Rio?

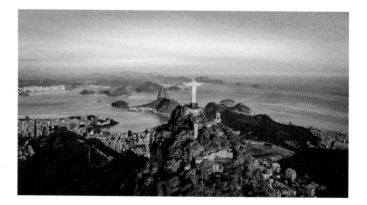

Bypass the whole 'Let me know if there is anything I or we can do' thing. You know what to do.

One afternoon when I was in high school, I came home and saw our neighbour, Niels, shovelling gravel in his driveway. I picked up a shovel and joined him. It was obvious he could do with some help – there was no reason for me to ask. A couple of years later my mother died, and a few days after that Niels and his wife, Rita, rang my doorbell: 'Come over and eat with us tonight.' It was that kind of street. You didn't ask if people needed something, you just gave them what they needed. The point is that, sometimes, there is no reason to ask if someone needs help – so just help.

In an article in *American Scientist*, social psychologist Aroldo Rodrigues, a colleague of Levine's at California State University, explains that it might be because of language and culture: 'There is an important word in Brazil: *simpático*. It refers to a range of desirable social qualities – to be friendly, nice, agreeable and good-natured, a person who is fun to be with and pleasant to deal with. It is a social quality. Brazilians want to be seen as *simpático*. And going out of one's way to assist strangers is part of this image.' The importance of *simpático* could also explain the high levels of kindness in Hispanic cities such as San José, Mexico City and Madrid.

The study also showed that in societies in which people walk very quickly, people offer help but in a less kind way. In Rio, people would walk after the person who has dropped the pen and hand it to them; in New York, people would yell that you had dropped your pen but keep walking away.

For Robert Levine, it doesn't make sense that the people of New York have a less kind nature than the people of Kolkata. What seems to matter is what we are taught and how our citizens act. In a time when more and more people are moving to cities, this raises the question of how we may all be kinder, even though our cities are becoming more densely populated.

People's willingness to help a stranger

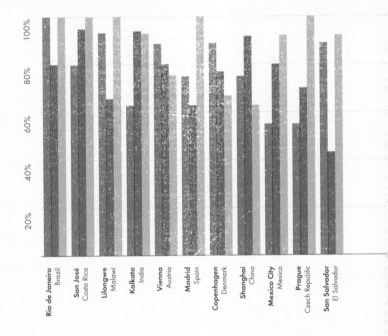

Source: Robert Levine, 'The Kindness of Strangers: People's Willingness to Help Someone during a Chance Encounter on a City Street Varies Considerably around the World', American Scientist, 2003

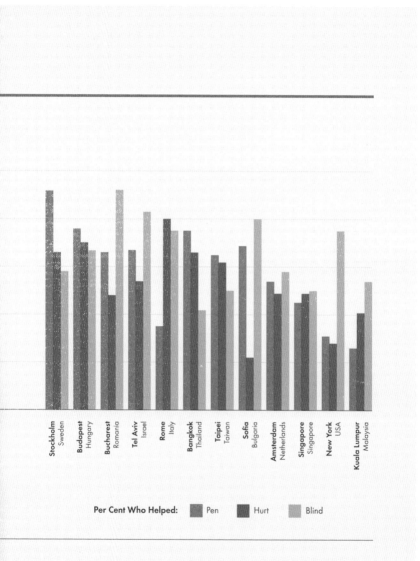

Per Cent Who Helped: ███ Pen ███ Hurt ░░░ Blind

FUCKING FRIENDLY

'Denmark is home to the happiest people on earth.
You'd think because we are the happiest, we would also
be the friendliest. We are not.'

Lars is the son of an American father and a Danish mother and the
founder of the Danish movement Fucking Flink. *Flink* is Danish for
'kind', 'nice', 'friendly', 'good-natured'.

In 2010, he published the book *Fucking Flink – How Do the Happiest
People in the World Also Become the Fucking Friendliest?* It is a sort
of 'friendliness manifesto' intended to provoke Danes into being
friendlier in their daily lives.

He is not trying to advocate more 'how are you?'s, 'please's and
'thank you's; what he is after is what he calls genuine friendliness,
caring about the people around you. Lars is one of the nicest people
I know. We have met a few times over the past years, and meeting
him always puts me in a good mood.

He believes that kindness breeds more kindness. 'But what I have
realized is that I am happier when I forget about myself and focus
on other people.' In one experiment, Lars pretended to be a parking
attendant but, instead of handing out tickets, he placed prizes on
the windshields of cars that had been parked considerately or were
excellent examples of parallel parking.

He knew that a book was not going to turn a nation of brute ex-
Vikings into champions of kindness, so he created a Facebook page
on which people could share stories of people doing nice things.

In 2012, it became the fastest growing Facebook page in Denmark, and it currently has 200,000 members – not bad for a nation of 5.5 million.

'I was in the supermarket on Rantzausgade in Copenhagen and noticed a couple in there with their son. He was about eight and had Down's syndrome. When I finished filling my basket, I went to the check-out and found the cashier on the customer side and in his seat the kid with Down's syndrome, who has the biggest smile on his face. He is scanning his parents' groceries. "Do you need anything else?" the kid asks his parents. After the parents had paid, their son handed them their receipt and high-fived the cashier. I left the store with the biggest smile and a warm feeling. I am so happy that there are people who are so fucking kind, that they take the time to do these kinds of things for other people.'

This is just one of thousands of stories which have been shared, inspiring more people to be kind and do more good: people driving other people home, children giving their toys to other children who look sad, and people reporting from a waiting room at the doctor's that they found wool, knitting needles and a half-knitted scarf with a note that read: 'Feel free to knit while you wait. When it is finished, we will give the scarf to a homeless person.'

Last year, Lars and his team conducted an experiment to explore the effects of being kind. The 981 people who participated were randomized into two groups. One was the control group, who would continue to act as before, and one was the treatment group, in which participants were asked to do one nice thing each day for a week. Before and after the experiment, all the participants were asked various questions about their well-being. The results showed that the people who had been performing kind acts for a week felt less angry, laughed more and felt more energized.

The participants also wrote down what they had done in terms of nice deeds. One woman in her forties wrote: 'The cashier at the supermarket was really surprised when I offered her a *flødebolle* (a chocolate-covered cream puff). It was *great*. She said yes. I had my kids, who are six and ten, with me, and after we left the shop they said, "That was fun, Mum. Can we do it again?" I felt I'd sown an important seed in my children that day.'

Lars is not the only one trying to make the world kinder and happier. In the UK, Action for Happiness is promoting kindness as one of the keys to happier living, and in the US the Random Acts of Kindness Foundation encourages people to become a 'RAKtivist' (Random Acts of Kindness activist) – a sort of kindness ambassador. I think most of us would like to help, but we are not always sure how we can, and we, like Clark, would like it to be personal.

There are also other platforms that are helping us help others. Be My Eyes is a Danish app that connects the blind and visually impaired with sighted helpers from around the world via a live video connection. It is free to download and free to use. Does this can contain corn or beans? Helpers help to distinguish between products, match or explain colours, find lost items and say whether lights are turned on or off. The app matches people based on language and time zone, so if you need help at 4 a.m. you don't need to worry that you're waking somebody up.

The app is used in 150 countries, with more than 35,000 blind and visually impaired individuals being assisted by more than 500,000 sighted helpers. In other words, for every one person needing help, fourteen people would like to help. It is testimony to how much people want to help if we give them the tools to do so, if we make it personal and if we connect them with people in need.

HAPPINESS TIP:
BECOME A RAKTIVIST

Start doing little Random Acts of Kindness

Sign up on the website www.randomactsofkindness.org and become a member of the Global Community of Kindness, or join local communities of kindness like the Fucking Flink movement (www.fuckingflink.dk/) in Denmark. Start out with little things: give a (sincere) compliment, help a tourist find their way, pass on a book you have enjoyed, tell someone who means a lot to you that they do.

KINDNESS

The Free Help Guy

London, UK: An anonymous man who will help with (almost) anything for free has found purpose and happiness in return. Read more on pp. 238–42.

The Gift Compassion Project

Hyderabad, India: Children from rich and poor schools are paired up and exchange gifts they have made themselves in order to break down social barriers.

Help for the Homeless

Warsaw, Poland: In a pillar-like chest of drawers in the middle of a square, homeless individuals have their own box, on which they write down the things they need the most. Caring passers-by can then drop the necessary items in the box.

Feeding man's best friend – and reducing waste

Istanbul, Turkey: To keep homeless dogs from starvation, the Turkish company Pugedon has invented a vending machine that dispenses dog food in exchange for bottles. When someone deposits a bottle at the top, food is released at the bottom. The Smart Recycling Boxes operate at no charge to the city and the recycled bottles cover the cost of the food.

The friendliest faces

Málaga, Spain: The Happiness Research Institute has been studying the frequency of smiles in the streets of more than twenty cities worldwide, and Málaga came out top. Read more on p. 256.

The kindest strangers

Rio de Janeiro, Brazil: Experiments to find out who will help a stranger pick up a pen that has been dropped or help blind people across the road have found Brazilians to be the kindest. Read more on pp. 260–61.

PUTTING THE PIECES TOGETHER

PUTTING THE
PIECES TOGETHER

'We love to complain.'

I was giving a presentation at Lille Catholic University in France and a member of the audience had an answer to the conundrum of why France ranks relatively low in the happiness rankings.

'The French love to complain,' he repeated.

'I guess we could try and quantify that,' I responded, and started to imagine how experiments on complaining could play out in the lab – possibly the coolest-sounding lab in the world: Laboratoire d'Anthropologie Expérimentale. Serving unsalted soup to people and monitoring how many bowls would be returned. Unfortunately, there have been no such studies. Yet.

However, a few weeks later, an Estonian told me, 'We have a great country in many ways, but Estonians, we love to complain.' Six months on, someone else tells me, 'We are Portuguese. We love to complain.'

Perhaps complaining is not a French thing, or an Estonian thing, or a Portuguese thing; perhaps it is a human thing. We all love to complain.

In fact, I think there should be a word for 'the joy of complaining', so let's invent one: *Beschwerdefreude*. Obviously, it has to be in German, a language that has not only given us words like *Weltschmerz* (literal meaning, 'world pain'; sadness caused by the

BESCH
WERDE
FREUDE

THE JOY OF
COMPLAINING*

*Not Really.

state of the world) and *Schadenfreude* (joy experienced when others are suffering) but also has a word for a present you give as an apology (*Drachenfutter* – literally, 'dragon fodder') and the feeling you get when you are getting older and fear that opportunities are slipping away (*Torschlusspanik*), and *Kopfkino* (literally, 'head cinema'; the act of playing out an entire scenario in your mind).

But why do we tend to zero in on the negative? Maybe we are negative because it makes us sound smarter. In her study 'Brilliant but Cruel', Teresa Amabile, a professor at Harvard Business School, asked people to evaluate the intelligence of book reviewers using reviews taken from the New York Times. Professor Amabile changed the reviews slightly, creating two different versions: one positive and one negative. She made only small changes in terms of the actual words, for example changing 'inspired' to 'uninspired' and 'capable' to 'incapable'.

A positive review might read, 'In 128 inspired pages, Alvin Harter, with his first work of fiction, shows himself to be an extremely capable young American author. A Longer Dawn is a novella – a prose poem, if you will – of tremendous impact. It deals with elemental things – life, love and death – and does so with such great intensity that it achieves new heights of superior writing on every page.'

While a negative review might read, 'In 128 uninspired pages, Alvin Harter, with his first work of fiction, shows himself to be an extremely incapable young American author. *A Longer Dawn* is a novella – a prose poem, if you will – of negligible impact. It deals with elemental things – life, love and death – and does so with such little intensity that it achieves new depths of inferior writing on every page.'

Half the people in the study read the first review, the other half read the second, and both rated the intelligence and expertise of the reviewer. Even though the reviews were almost identical – the only difference being whether they were positive or negative – people considered the reviewers with negative versions 14 per cent more intelligent and as having 16 per cent more expertise in literature. Professor Amabile writes that 'prophets of doom and gloom appear wise and insightful'. Anyone can say something nice – but it takes an expert to critique it.

So, we may complain because we want to appear smarter, but we may also be hard-wired to zoom in on negative or bad events for reasons of evolution. Species that are better at remembering incidents that have led to danger would be more likely to survive. For example, running across a sabre-toothed tiger means bad news. Most of us remember criticism far better than we remember praise. I did well in school, but the only thing I remember a teacher telling me word for word is my PE teacher saying that I had absolutely no talent for sports. PE teacher means bad news.

... why do we tend to zero in on the negative? Maybe we are negative because it makes us sound smarter.

COLLECTING AND
CONNECTING THE PIECES

I understand that remembering the positive, focusing on the positive and finding out what works for us may not come naturally.

And I realize that doing these things may make me look foolish. But to me it would be foolish not to notice when a man turns kindness into happiness or when a woman discovers a well-being beyond material wealth. And once we have gathered enough pieces of evidence, we might start to see a connection between these things.

These sorts of kindness foster a spirit of trust and cooperation. Building a community garden may improve both our health and our sense of connection. Freedom is organizing our lives so that our happiness does not depend on how much we earn. All the factors that explain why some people are happier than others are connected. I believe that if we put these pieces together, we may not only write a happier chapter in our own lives to come but also build a better tomorrow for those who will follow us.

Some places have already put the pieces together, either knowingly or by chance. One of these is Todmorden in Yorkshire. Until recently, there was nothing unusual about the place. Fifty thousand people live here; the Industrial Revolution had come and gone.

But around ten years ago, a group of citizens sparked a revolution. One of them was Pam Warhurst, a businesswoman and former council leader in Todmorden.

'"Who is up for changing the world with local food?" we asked, and we held a meeting in a café. Sixty people came. After a bit of talking, one got up and said, "Let's just get on with it. We can grow. We can share. We can cook. No need to write a report or talk more about it. Let's just get on with it." And the whole room exploded. And from that moment, I knew we were on to something.' That was the beginning of Incredible Edible.

Today, plant beds, fruit trees and vegetable patches seem to occupy every free space around the town. Outside the police station, the fire station, the parking lots, the train station, the cemetery. Yes, the cemetery – they say the soil is extremely good there.

The message is the same for everyone: take some – it's free.

Every school grows vegetables and fruit. The kids helped to build the vegetable garden by the school, and the school now teaches agriculture. The initiative is changing the way the pupils think about food and health. They call it propaganda gardening. They have found the language that unifies us: a language that cuts across age, gender and culture.

Everybody has to eat. It is about food, obviously, but it is also about finding common ground that enables everybody to come together. Talking about food was just a simple way to unite people. People wanted to do something, but they were not sure what to do.

In Todmorden, everybody can play a role in this project. Their motto is: If you eat – you're in. Some grow, some design the signs for the vegetable beds, some cook. You can be a regular or be on the 'muck-in' list: hundreds are contacted if there is a special event and extra hands are needed.

Incredible Edible is built on three fronts: community, education and business. The community part is how the people there live their everyday lives. The educational element is what they teach the kids in school and what skills they can share and teach each other. The business aspect is what they do with the pounds in their pockets and which businesses they choose to support.

They have created economic confidence locally and invented a new sort of tourism: vegetable tourism. They have increased the share of locally produced food in the shops, and 49 per cent of food sellers say their bottom line has increased because of Incredible Edible initiatives. They have launched the campaign 'Every Egg Matters', to encourage people to keep chickens and sell their eggs locally. An online map shows where they are being sold. They started with four local producers; now they have more than sixty.

Whether it is three fronts or six factors of happiness, they all seem to be mutually reinforcing. And Todmorden has done it all without a single strategy document, without a single penny of government support. And the initiative is spreading throughout the UK and throughout the world.

In more than a hundred places, people have stopped thinking of themselves only as customers and have begun to act as citizens. In more than a hundred places, people are rethinking how we can reshape our communities and our lives. In more than a hundred places, people are proving what cultural anthropologist Margaret Mead believed:

> *'Never doubt that a small group of thoughtful, committed citizens can change the world; indeed, it's the only thing that ever has.'*

USE THE BUILDING BLOCKS

Combine the six factors with each other.

By now, you have an advantage in developing ideas about how to help people, about how to show more kindness and make the world a happier place – your world and everybody else's. Combine kindness with the five other factors we have been looking at in this book. You may try kind togetherness, for example: invite someone new in town for dinner. You may spend kind money: think about where and for whom an additional ten pounds may bring most happiness. You may show healthy kindness: do a run for a good cause. Offer someone a night of freedom by helping them out with babysitting or by cooking meals they can put in their freezer. Develop trust by being the kind stranger who makes someone believe that there is still good in this world. In other words, start putting the pieces together.

BE MY EYES

The aim of this book is not to belittle the challenges we face. I am painfully aware of the struggles of many, how difficult times are and how big the stakes for much of humanity.

But these are not the days when we can afford to reach for fear, mistrust and cynicism. That will never bring us towards a happier place.

What will bring us forward is a spirit of trust and cooperation and the realization that we are each other's keepers. What will bring us forward is being freed of fear and showing kindness to strangers. What will bring us forward is redesigning our cities to ensure health and happiness and removing the price tag on quality of life.

Now is the time to look for the good in the world – and, for that, I need your help.

My aim in this book was to take you on a treasure hunt, and I hope you will agree that we have uncovered some caskets of happiness gold. But I also hope you will agree that there are so many more out there to be found.

For that, I need you to be my eyes, to continue this pursuit of happiness. To show the good that does exist in this world and to bring it into the light so that, together, we can help it spread.

Let's put a positive spin on the phrase 'If you see something, say something.' If you see something that increases the happiness of you, your community or the world as a whole, talk about it, write about it, film it, photograph it – and pass it on.

At the Happiness Research Institute, we will be following the hashtag #Look4Lykke on social media. Tell us what works when it comes to improving quality of life. In what ways are people and societies paving the way to happiness? We are looking for micro-libraries, community gardens and all those things which we may have had no idea even exist. We are listening to the people and the ideas that have a positive impact on you and on our world.

Most importantly, find out how you can have a positive impact on your world. On our world. We need more dreamers and doers. We need more creators of kindness, heroes of happiness and champions of change.

This is the outlook that each and every one of us needs and can feed into.

The way the world is going, some might call this false hope – but there has never been anything false about hope.

And remember: there is no point in being a pessimist – that shit never works anyway.

PHOTO CREDITS

ABOUT THE AUTHOR

Meik Wiking is the CEO of the Happiness Research Institute in Copenhagen and is one of the world's leading experts in happiness. Committed to understanding happiness, subjective well-being and quality of life, Meik works with countries across the world to discover and explore global trends of life satisfaction. Only someone absolutely dedicated to happiness sits in coffee shops across the world counting people's smiles!

His first book, *The Little Book of Hygge*, became an international bestseller and will soon be available in thirty-one countries.

THANKS

Thanks to Kjartan Andsbjerg, Kirsten Frank, Cindie Unger, Rannvá Pállson Joensen, Maria Risvig, Gabe Rudin, Marie Louise Dornoy, Teis Rasmussen, Michael Mærsk-Møller, Marie Lundby, Lisa Magelund, Morten Tromholt, Michael Birkjær, Johan Jansen, Felicia Öberg, Maria Stahmer Humlum, Marie Lange Hansen, Lydia Kirchner, Jacob Fischer, Vanessa Zaccaria, Isabella Arendt and Xavier Landes.

Always hire people who are smarter than you. For me, those are easy to find, but they have also been good people who believe in building a better world and have helped me shape this book and the Happiness Research Institute.